Contact Information for Larry Foster, ✍ **W9-CTH-505**

Mail: Doctor Divot Publishing, Inc.
P.O. Box 436
North Salem, NY 10560

E-Mail: doctordivotmd@aol.com
Phone/fax: **(845) 279-0667**
Website: www.doctordivotmd.com

Dr. Divot's
Guide to
Golf Injuries

Dr. Divot's Guide to Golf Injuries is available through:

- **Direct from-the-publisher purchase: 1-(800) 247-6553**
  (50% discount   to pro shops, teaching pros, trainers, physical
  therapists, and corporate/charity golf outings)

- **The Booklegger: 1-(800) 262-1556** (Ask for catalog item
  #2093)

- **Website purchase:** www.doctordivotmd.com

- **Amazon.com**

Dr. Divot's Guide to Golf Injuries

A Handbook for Golf Injury Prevention and Treatment

Larry Foster, M.D., F.A.A.O.S.
"Dr. Divot, M.D."

DOCTOR DIVOT
PUBLISHING, INC.
North Salem, NY

Interior graphic art by Moki Kokoris

Although the author and publisher have made every effort to ensure the accuracy and completeness of information contained in this book, we assume no responsibility for errors, inaccuracies, omissions, or any inconsistency herein. Any slights of people, places, or organizations are unintentional.

As new scientific information becomes available through basic and clinical research, recommended treatments and therapies undergo changes. The author and publisher have done everything possible to make this book accurate, up to date, and in keeping with accepted standards at the time of publication. The author and publisher of this book make no warranty, expressed or implied, in regard to the contents of the book. Any advice or practice described in this book should applied by the reader according to the reader's unique circumstances. Caution is especially urged when considering the use of medication or exercises. The reader is reminded that his own physician should be consulted before adopting any new medication or exercise regimen.

First printing 2004

ISBN 0-9747315-4-4
LCCN 2003114982

ATTENTION CORPORATIONS, UNIVERSITIES, COLLEGES, AND PROFESSIONAL ORGANIZATIONS: Quantity discounts are available on bulk purchases of this book for educational, gift purposes, or as premiums for increasing magazine subscriptions or renewals. Special books or book excerpts can also be created to fit specific needs. For information, please contact Doctor Divot Publishing, Inc., P.O. Box 436, North Salem, NY 10560.

TABLE OF CONTENTS

"FORE"-WORD   ix

ACKNOWLEDGMENTS   xiii

HOW TO USE THIS BOOK   xv

CHAPTER 1
Introduction to Golf Injuries   1

CHAPTER 2
The Frequency of Golf Injuries   7

CHAPTER 3
The Golf Swing and Injury   15

CHAPTER 4
Sprains, Strains, Fractures, and Tendonitis in Golf   21

CHAPTER 5
Elbow Injuries   35

CHAPTER 6
Wrist and Hand Injuries   55

CHAPTER 7
Back Pain and Spine Injuries   77

CHAPTER 8
Shoulder Injuries   105

CHAPTER 9
Knee Injuries   123

CHAPTER 10
The Golf Warm-Up   137

CHAPTER 11
Conditioning and Preventive Exercises for Golf   149

CHAPTER 12
The Female Golfer   167

CHAPTER 13
The Older Golfer   177

CHAPTER 14
Joint Replacement and the Golfer   185

Golf Injury Roundup—Putting It All Together   201

RECOMMENDED READING   211

REFERENCES   213

INDEX   219

"FORE"-WORD

Contrary to popular belief, all doctors are not expert golfers. If a low handicap was a prerequisite for being a physician, then my AMA membership card would have been confiscated long ago. Sadly, all my years of toil and sacrifice in medical school and residency did nothing for my golf game—except that Brian my golfing buddy calls me "Dr. Divot, M.D." when we're out hacking up the course. To us, it's a good day of golf when the beer stays cold through the eighteenth and nobody's been hurt.

The purpose of this book, then, is not to teach you the fine points of golf technique. Thousands of such books, written by qualified golf pros and gurus, are already available. Besides, learning to play golf from me would be like learning from a rock how to swim. Rather, my goal is help you gain a better understanding of a little-discussed topic in golf—the *diagnosis, treatment, and prevention of golf injuries*. Furthermore, playing the game can aggravate *nongolf* injuries. As a Board Certified orthopedic surgeon, I shall focus on injuries to the musculoskeletal system—that is, injuries to the bones, joints, muscles, tendons, ligaments, and nerves.

I first became interested in the topic of orthopedic injuries in golf in 1993 while in my final year of residency training at the Hospital for Joint Diseases in New York City. Each graduating resident was required to give a lecture to the other residents and attending physicians. At the time, I had only played golf once or twice in my life. Most of the other residents, however, were already victims of the golf bug and talked about the game constantly. So, I figured that topic would keep at least some of the audience awake until the lights came back on.

Not everyone was thrilled with my choice of subject, however. When my department chairman, Dr. Joseph Zuckerman, heard what I planned to lecture on, he immediately called me to his office and told me in no uncertain terms—with a few expletives thrown in for good measure—to choose a "serious" medical topic instead. It was a tough sell, but I finally convinced him that orthopedic injury in golf *was* a serious topic, and he grudgingly agreed to let me give my presentation. Well, the lecture was a hit with my colleagues, and I even got a pat on the back from Dr. Zuckerman.

After completing my orthopedic training, I moved out of New York City and fell victim to the golf bug myself. Now I play—poorly—whenever I can. In my orthopedic practice I've encountered numerous golfers, from recreational players to local pros, who have sought treatment for injuries either caused by golf or made worse by playing the game. As a golfer, I've experienced my own collection of aches and pains, and as more and more golfers came to me for treatment, I was reminded of that lecture I gave years ago. If other doctors, I reasoned, had found the topic of golf injuries interesting, perhaps *nonphysicians* would as well. A visit to the local bookstore and a check of the Internet confirmed that even though there were tons of books about golf (how-to books, exercise books, diet books, even cartoon books) there was not much about golf injuries at all.

Who needs a book on golf injuries? Just about all of us. There are about 25 million golfers in the United States alone, and in the book *Break 100 Now!* authors Mike Adams and T. J. Tomasi estimate that fully 80 percent of the golfers out there fail to break 100 on a regular basis. (I know, I was a little bit in over my head in buying their book, but the store didn't have one titled "Break 130 Now!") As you shall discover later in this book, poor swing technique is one of several major risk factors for golf injury. Let's see. . . 80 percent of 25 million. . . Wow, that's 20 million duffers! Twenty million guys and gals at risk for injury due to poor swing technique alone. I am indeed in good company. Furthermore, older athletes are more prone to injury than younger athletes. Add to that the fact that more than one in four golfers is over the age of fifty, and the need to discuss the role of injury in golf becomes even more clear (32).

Inspired, I dusted off my old lecture notes and began to re-search the current medical literature. Although there is a substantial body of medical knowledge and research dedicated to golf and golf-related injuries, the books and journal articles I reference in the following chapters were written by doctors for other medical professionals to read.

Because the language of medicine takes years to learn and therefore remains foreign to most people, I view myself, writing this book, as a "translator" of sorts. My goal is to survey the information available in the medical literature and to present it in a way that is easy for the *nonphysician* to understand and use. I have purposely kept the medical jargon to a minimum. Readers who have medical training (physical therapists or trainers, for example, and even doctors) are certainly encouraged to look up the original articles and books listed in the References, but they will also find this book's special focus on the popular sport of golf a useful review.

My years in medicine have taught me that the best doctors are the ones who are the best teachers. I always take the time to explain things to my patients in plain English, so that they fully understand their injury and the rationale behind my treatment recommendations. I hope that reading this book helps you to understand why the most common golf injuries occur and what you can do to prevent them. And if you do become injured, this book will give you a head start in discussing with your own doctor, and your local golf pro, what steps can be taken to treat your injury and rehabilitate you. By staying pain-free and in-jury-free, you are bound to have more fun on the golf course. As I said, a good day of golf is when the beer stays cold and nobody gets hurt.

Larry Foster, M.D., F.A.A.O.S.
(Dr. Divot, M.D.)

DEDICATION

To my wife, Patty,
who somehow manages to both
put up with me and love me.

To my "monkeys," Lawrence and Claire,
who are my pride and joy.

To my father, the best writer I know.

To my mother, the kindest person I know.

To my siblings, Cindi, David, Nanci, and Gregg,
who are my best friends.

ACKNOWLEDGMENTS

It is my hope that the admittedly irreverent tone of this book in no way detracts from the seriousness of the science—and the sport—that it describes. Many dedicated researchers have spent years designing and implementing the studies cited in this book. Some might argue that their time might be better spent studying more weighty medical issues, but I disagree.

Golf is a serious sport for many hundreds of professionals. More important, golf is a way of life for *millions* of the rest of us. Golf gives us fun and camaraderie. It provides an opportunity for exercise in pleasant and friendly surroundings, and it gives us some time away from our crazy lives. Golf brings generations together in a way that few pastimes can. Golf is even crucial to the machinations of modern-day business wheeling and dealing. So, what could be wrong with trying to learn more about the science behind the game we all love so much?

This book is unique in that it is written like many academic papers. I have purposely placed the pertinent references throughout the text in order to give proper credit to the researchers whose work I have "translated." Two important contributing bodies of work deserve special mention. The first is the January 1996 issue of the orthopedic journal *Clinics in Sports Medicine*, which focused solely on golf. That such a prestigious medical journal would devote and entire issue to the subject indicates that sports medicine physicians consider it a quite legitimate topic. The second key resource is the book *Feeling Up to Par: Medicine from Tee to Green*, edited by Cornelius Stover, M.D.,

John McCarroll, M.D., and William Mallon, M.D.—three ortho-pedic surgeons who are experts in golf-related injuries.

This book would not be possible were it not for the aca-demic efforts of these and the many other authors cited in the references. They have written articles and chapters brimming with fascinating scientific inquiries and eloquent conclusions. To all these scholars I am indebted, and I am honored and humbled to consider them my colleagues.

I would also like to thank my family, friends, and colleagues for their support and insights. Special thanks also to Peggy Hoover for her wonderful editing and to Moki Kokoris, Suzanne AuBuchon, and Mark Bremmer for their beautiful artwork. Thanks also to Tom Nieporte for sharing his wisdom as a tour-ing pro, teacher, and lover of the game.

HOW TO USE THIS BOOK

The best way to get the most out of this book is to read it from cover to cover. No, there won't be a riveting cloak-and-dagger plot to follow, but each chapter *does* build on and rely somewhat on information provided in previous chapters. This even includes things mentioned in the "Fore"-word and Acknowledgments. If you skipped those—I don't think I have ever read a foreword to a book in my life—go back and read them now. I'll wait. . .

Because I am discussing medical issues for laypeople, nonphysicians, there will be times when I have to define a word or explain a term. Repeating those definitions and explanations in chapter after chapter would drive both you and me nutty, so if you read the chapters in order there's less chance for confusion.

You could use this book like a reference book—reading the elbow chapter if your elbow is sore, or the knee chapter if you injured your knee. But again, I'd recommend that you read the whole book through completely, once—that should only take a few hours. This way, you'll be more likely to absorb the most important themes in the book about *injury prevention.* I'd much rather be coaching you on how to prevent injuries than be treating injuries that could have been prevented. After your first complete reading, you can go back and review specific chapters as needed.

It is important to remember that the diagnosis and treatment of medical conditions can be complicated—certainly more complicated than they may appear in the following chapters. ***This book is not intended as a substitute for appropriate medical care by your own physician.*** If you become injured, my goal is to provide you with basic medical and biomechanical knowledge that will help you work with your own physician and therapist to reach a speedier resolution of the problem. Furthermore, the information I provide about swing mechanics can serve as a starting point for discussion between you and your local golf pro to work out any technique flaws that may be causing or aggravating an injury. There is an old saying that any lawyer who represents himself has a fool for a client. The same is true for a person who acts as his or her own doctor.

The medical information in the following chapters does not necessarily represent the only, or even the best, way of treating the injuries I discuss. Each doctor relies on his or her own unique experience and training to prescribe what he or she feels is best for the patient. You may also find regional variations in treatment approaches. The treatment options I outline are therefore by no means a complete list—they reflect my experience as a practicing community orthopedist as well as the opinions of the authors of the medical literature I cite. So, please don't be upset if I do not mention such treatment options as chiropractic or acupuncture for back pain, for example. I am not sufficiently familiar with such treatment methods to comment on them fairly. I do know that there is more than one way to skin a cat. The way I see it, whatever treatment works for you and gets you back out on the golf course *safely* is okay with me.

Introduction to Golf Injuries

Being a doctor is like belonging to a select club or fraternity. We speak our own special language (no secret handshake, though). We get to put lots of letters after our names (very impressive). We even get our own special license plates and parking spaces—all pretty neat stuff. Doctors also have a reputation for being somewhat snooty and aloof—not good. To show you that I'm just a regular guy (as if calling myself "Dr. Divot, M.D." weren't enough to prove my humility), I'm going to share with you a glimpse of my private world—my often pathetic but bittersweet world of golf.

To many of you, the following scenario may sound strangely familiar. As you read along, see if you can spot the ways recreational golfers—that's you and me—commonly place themselves at risk for injury.

A typical day of golf for me starts early. The kids may be up watching Rugrats reruns on TV, but my wife is usually still asleep. I try not to wake her. If I did, she might say "Have fun!" But then again, maybe not. Better to let her sleep. With a list in hand of things for me to do around the house, she'll have plenty to say when I get home. (It's really marriage maintenance more than home maintenance, the way I see it.) If I'm running on time, which is rare, I'll pop in the deli to grab a coffee and a bacon-egg-and-cheese on a roll. (I'm a bone doctor, not a cardiologist,

1

you know.) More often, I am driving like a maniac just to make my tee time.

At the course, I'll meet up with my brother Gregg or my buddy Brian. I play golf with these guys not only because I love them, but also because they stink at golf every bit as much as I do, and misery loves company. At this time of day it's usually chilly, and even downright frosty at some times of year. In the parking lot, we toss our golf shoes on, grab a cart, and zoom off to the first tee. The "warm-up" consists of blowing into my hands, grabbing my driver from my bag, and taking two or three practice swings.

I hate it when other golfers are standing around watching as I get set to hit the ball. It's even worse when we only have a twosome and get paired up with two guys we don't know—too much pressure to hit a good first shot. When I do hit that inevitable first dribbler, I can hear the poor guys who got stuck with us groaning to themselves. But I put on an Academy Award performance, appearing shocked and indignant at my mis-hit— as if such a thing *never* happened to me before. The truth is, I had honed that very shot dozens of times the week before at the driving range. Abraham Lincoln once said, "Better to remain silent and be thought a fool than to speak out and remove all doubt." Unfortunately, with golf there's no faking it. If you stink, it soon shows.

As we plod along the course, the saga unfolds. A good shot here—even a blind squirrel finds a nut once in a while—three bad shots there. Ecstasy—agony—par—quadruple bogey. Shots so far into the woods I have to leave a trail of breadcrumbs so I can find my way back to the fairway. Up and down so many hills that I begin to wonder if they make golf carts with four-wheel drive.

To our credit, at least we don't play for money. The one time we tried that was a fiasco. We were outwardly celebrating every time the other guy missed a shot—instead of inwardly celebrating, like we do all the other times.

The beauty of the setting takes hold as the day proceeds. There's the fresh air, the sunshine, the trees, the rocks. Ah, the trees and the rocks. I'm convinced that some prankster in the X-out department at the ball factory sneaks some sort of tree-rock homing device into the balls destined for my bag. If I'm not hacking away at the base of some poor tree like Paul Bunyan, I'm launching clods of turf farther down the fairway than my ball usually goes.

The round ends in the clubhouse with a few beers and a bad hot dog. We go over in great detail all the good shots of the day, which takes all of thirty seconds or so, and spend the rest of the time making fun of one another.

I am not sure why, but I find this golfing thing to be fun, *really* fun. Even though while I'm playing I spend half the time cursing like a sailor, I always leave with a warm feeling in my heart—or is that just the bad hot dog I'm feeling?

By the time I get home, though, my back has stiffened up on me so much that I walk into the house like an old man. I don't look for sympathy from my spouse, because there isn't any to be had. She knows I had my fun. What does await me is a generous helping of marriage maintenance, and it's all worth it. All kidding aside, though, my wife is a good sport about my golf habit.

The purpose of this little exposé of my golfing life is to point out many of the factors that can lead to injury in the average golfer. Though I hope that professionals and low-handicap players find this book useful, it is really written with the average golfer in mind. Instead of covering every type of injury that can be related to golf, this book focuses on musculoskeletal injuries sustained during play.

While a story of some guy who accidentally impales himself on his club after breaking it in a fit of rage makes for interesting talk on the way to the next tee, I don't focus on rare or freak accidents, but rather on injuries derived primarily from swinging the club at the ball. Specifically, the focus of this book is injuries that occur from swinging the club *too often* or swinging it the *wrong way*.

The act of swinging a golf club, regardless of how far or straight the ball goes, is an extremely demanding sports activity. The action places significant stresses on the body, and in order to develop club head speeds that can exceed 100 miles an hour in less than one-fifth of a second, muscles and joints are stressed near their limits (7). Experts in golf medicine note that it is a *combination* of a number of factors that contribute to amateur golfer injuries. Some of these factors are *poor physical conditioning, overuse (excessive play or practice), failure to warm up adequately, and poor swing technique* (5)(31).

I'm sure you've heard the saying "Physician, heal thyself." Well, let's see if I can figure out just why my back feels like it's been run over by the bulls at Pamplona after I play golf. Take a middle-aged golf nut who couldn't run three miles if his life depended on it (me). Next, send him to a driving range so he can practice his lousy golf swing over and over and over (me, again). Now, on a chilly morning have him jump from the car to the tee without warming up properly (me again, *sometimes*). And just for good measure, let's take a few dozen pothole-sized divots and whack a few rocks and trees while we are out there (me, always).

So, it's not just bad luck that causes golfing injuries, especially in the amateur. Put it all together and it starts to make sense. For the amateur golfer, injuries are all too often due to:

- Poor physical conditioning
- Overuse (excessive play or practice)
- Inadequate or improper warm-up
- Poor swing technique

Figure 1-1.
Doctor Divot's *recipe for injury* for the amateur golfer. (Illustration by Moki Kokoris)

So, my personal *recipe for injury* includes a pinch of overuse, a dash of poor conditioning, a smidgen of improper warm-up, and four heaping tablespoons of poor technique. I'm probably not going too far out on a limb to suggest that some or all of these risk factors for injury that *I* have apply to you as well. Come on, don't be ashamed to admit it. There are *millions* of us out there!

The good news is that these factors are for the most part within the control of the amateur golfer. Rather than dealing with a painful injury after it occurs, doesn't it make a lot more sense to *avoid* injury in the first place? Say "Yes, Dr. Divot, M.D., teach me more."

Well, you might be surprised to find out how many golfers are getting hurt out there. In the next chapter we look at the frequency of golf injuries.

Note that as you read through the book you will come across numbered references in parentheses sprinkled about the text. These refer to the original medical articles and chapters I used to help me write the book. Interested readers can use the References section in the back of the book to track down the original medical literature.

The Frequency of Golf Injuries

Golf injuries occur with surprising frequency to both the professional and the amateur player. What you read here should quell the notion that golf is a cushy "gentleman's" pastime. We start by looking at the overall frequency of golf injuries for both pros and amateurs, then turn to which specific body areas are most often involved.

Golf Injuries in Professionals

Until I began to play golf myself several years ago, I never really appreciated how hard golf can be on a person's body. It's really quite a strenuous game. Watching professionals play so well with so little visible effort on television is misleading: the true rigors of the game are not apparent. Several revealing articles in the medical literature provide insight into just how frequently the elite, professional players sustain injuries from golfing. Most of the data come from surveys of the pros themselves (1)(6)(31)(34). You may be surprised to learn that:

- More than 80 percent of professional golfers reported a golf-related injury at some point in their career.
- An estimated 10 percent to 33 percent of professional golfers are playing while injured at any given time.
- Pros average nearly two injuries during their career.

- The average time lost from touring due to an injury is more than nine weeks for men and nearly three weeks for women.
- When the injured pros do return to the tour, nearly half are still bothered by their injuries, but return nonetheless.

We all envy golf professionals—I wouldn't mind a crack at being a rock star for a little while either—but even the most naturally gifted among these elite players still put in countless hours of practice and preparation. A typical day for the pro golfer includes hitting up to 300 full shots on the range, completing several hours of putting practice, and taking a practice round on the golf course—a total of about 10 hours toiling in the sun (31).

Professional golfers not only swing the club many times a day, they also swing it in a very demanding way. A majority of professional and low-handicap golfers employ a so-called "modern" swing technique in which maximum coiling of the body's trunk is combined with an explosive downswing and hyperextension of the spine on the follow-through to produce optimum club head speed and power. And most experts believe that injuries to the professional golfer stem primarily from the relentless repetition demanded by their practice and competition schedules (7)(32).

In one survey of hundreds of professional golfers, the relative frequencies of injury to various body parts were tabulated (see Figure 2-1) (6):

- Among the professional males, injuries occurred most often to the lower back (25 percent of all male injuries), the left wrist (16 percent), and the left shoulder (11 percent).
- Among the professional females, injuries occurred most often to the left wrist (31 percent of all female injuries), the lower back (22 percent), and the left hand (8 percent).

- When combining data for professional males and females, injuries occurred most often to the back (24 percent of all professional injuries), the wrist (24 percent), the hand (7 percent), and the left shoulder (7 percent).

The two most common causes for injury reported by this group of professional golfers were (A) overpractice or overrepetitive swings, and (B) contact with an object other than the ball during a swing (for example, the ground or a rock).

From a purely scientific standpoint, surveys are not the best way to gather data for research on injuries. Because survey participation is voluntary, results may be inaccurate because some golfers who have been injured may not have been included in the study. However, surveys are the best method available for understanding the frequency of golf injuries. Other surveys may yield differing injury frequencies (1)(6)(31)(32)(34).

What is most important, therefore, is to get a general feeling for where most golf-related injuries occur. The take-home message from all the surveys I have read is that golfing results in a strikingly high rate of injury for those who play professionally.

So, while we may envy the professional golfer for his or her seemingly glamorous life spent jetting from one lush paradise to the next, we are reminded that these athletes are frequently playing in pain. Nonetheless, though injured, they are obligated to put in many long hours working at something that you and I do solely for the pure fun of it.

GOLF INJURIES
Professionals

Figure 2-1. Golf injuries—professionals. This figure shows the most frequently reported sites of injury in a study of professional golfers who responded to a survey (6). The results are for male and female professional golfers combined. Other injury sites included the ankle/foot (5 percent) and the neck (3 percent).

Some important things to note:

- Injuries to the lower back are very common.
- Injuries to the upper limbs (shoulder, elbow, wrist, and hand) account for more than half the total number of injuries. The majority of these injuries occur to the *left* (lead) side of the body
- Injuries to the lower limbs (hip, knee, ankle, and foot) are relatively uncommon, accounting for only about 10 percent of the total injuries.

Some important differences between male and female professional golfers include:

- For males, the most frequently injured sites include the lower back (25 percent), left wrist (16 percent), and left shoulder (11 percent).

WRIST / HAND (37%)
LOW BACK (24%)
SHOULDER (10%)
ELBOW (7%)
KNEE (7%)

- Among females, the most commonly injured areas include the left wrist (31 percent), the lower back (22 percent), and the left hand (8 percent).

Keep in mind that the exact numbers of each type of injury may vary from one survey to another. What is most important is getting a general feeling for where most golf-related injuries occur. (Illustration by Moki Kokoris)

Golf Injuries in Amateurs

Several large-scale surveys of amateur golfers confirm that injuries to the lowly hacker are also common (and keep in mind that most golfers *are* hackers). One survey of more than 1,000 amateurs (4) revealed the following:

- More than 60 percent of the amateur golfers sustained one or more golf-related injuries over the course of their playing years. (No, a "bruised ego" does not count as an injury—otherwise we would *all* be considered having been injured on the golf course.)
- The injury rate was higher for amateur players over the age of fifty (a 65 percent injury rate) than it was for players younger than fifty (58 percent injury rate).
- The injury rate was slightly higher—67.5 percent among low-handicap amateur golfers (handicap less than 9)—than it was for less-skilled amateur golfers.
- The typical injury forced the amateur golfer to miss an average of more than five weeks of playing time.
- The injury rates for male and female amateur golfers were about the same.

Other surveys of amateurs (5)(32) may provide slightly different statistics, but the overall message is clear: Amateur golfers get hurt playing golf—a lot!

In one survey, the relative frequencies of injury to various body parts of amateurs were tabulated (see Figure 2-2) (4).

- Among the amateur males, injuries occurred most often to the lower back (36 percent of all male injuries), the elbow (33 percent), the wrist or hand (21 percent), the shoulder (11 percent), and the knee (9 percent).
- Among the females, injuries occurred most often to the elbow (36 percent of all female injuries), the lower back (27 percent), the shoulder (16 percent), the wrist or hand (15 percent), and the knee (11 percent).
- When combining data for the males and females, injuries occurred most often to the lower back (35 percent of all amateur injuries), the elbow (33 percent), the wrist or

Figure 2-2. Golf injuries–amateurs. This figure shows the most frequently reported sites of injury in a study of amateur golfers who responded to a survey (4). The results are for male and female amateur golfers combined. Other injury sites included the ankle/foot (3 percent) and the neck (3 percent).

Some important things to note:

- Injuries to the lower back are very common to amateurs too.

- Injuries to the upper limbs (shoulder, elbow, wrist, and hand) account for more than half the total injuries in amateurs too. Again, the majority of these upper limb injuries occur to the *left* (lead) side.

- The frequency of elbow injuries is much *higher* for the amateur player than it is for the professional.

- Injuries to the lower limbs (hip, knee, ankle, and foot) are relatively uncommon for amateurs too, accounting for only about 10 percent of the total injuries.

Some important differences between male and female amateur golfers include:

GOLF INJURIES
Amateurs

LOW BACK (35%)
ELBOW (33%)
WRIST / HAND (20%)
SHOULDER (12%)
KNEE (9%)

- For males, the most frequently injured sites include the lower back (36 percent), the elbow (33 percent), and the wrist/hand (21 percent).

- Among females, the most commonly injured areas include the elbow (36 percent), the lower back (27 percent), and the shoulder (16 percent).

Keep in mind that the exact numbers of each type of injury may vary from one survey to another. What is most important is getting a general feeling for where most golf-related injuries occur. (Illustration by Moki Kokoris) hand (20 percent), the shoulder (12 percent), and the knee (9 percent).

Notice that the body areas injured among amateurs tend to parallel those in the professionals, with one major exception: Amateur golfers are much more prone to elbow injury than professionals are.

As with the professionals, lower-limb injuries to amateurs are relatively rare. Hip, knee, and ankle injuries together account for only about 10 percent of the total (31).

The three most common causes for injury reported by this group of amateur golfers were:

- Excessive play or practice
- Poor swing mechanics
- Hitting the ground or an object during a swing

Professional golfers have superior conditioning and swing technique that protect them from injury. As we have seen, professionals usually sustain their injuries from the sheer number of swings they take each week. But why do amateurs get hurt playing golf? We aren't professionals. We don't practice 10 hours a day, as the pros do.

Ah, but we *do* practice. And furthermore, our swing mechanics are often faulty, placing more strain on our (out-of-shape) bodies than professionals, with their more efficient "grooved" swing, experience. Now, throw in the fact that amateurs tend to neglect the importance of a proper warm-up routine, and you have the recipe for injury. Therefore, for the poorly conditioned amateur, the overpracticing of a golf swing chock-full of technical deficiencies makes for a dangerous combination (1)(4)(31)(32).

One interesting survey compared the characteristics of injured amateur golfers with those of their noninjured counterparts (33) and found that golfers who sustained golfing injuries tended to play more rounds per week, were less likely to have taken golf lessons, and admitted to feeling more fatigue after golfing.

The authors of the study conclude that improving the overall fitness level of the amateur, and improving swing technique, might decrease the risk of injury.

Parting Shots:
Golf Injuries

More than eight out of ten professional golfers report a golf-related injury that has forced them to miss a significant time away from competition.

Up to one in three professional golfers are playing while injured at any given time.

Professional golfers sustain most of their injuries from the high number of swings their busy play and practice schedules demand. Mis-hits also cause injury.

The lower back and the upper limbs (shoulder, elbow, wrist/hand) are frequent sites of injury in the professional.

More than six out of ten amateur golfers report a golf-related injury.

Injuries among amateurs increase with age.

The sites and frequencies of golf injuries among amateurs generally parallel those among professionals. Amateur golfers, however, experience a significantly higher rate of injury to the elbow.

Injuries to both professional and amateur golfers occur predominantly on the left (lead) side.

Overuse (excessive play or practice), poor conditioning, inadequate warm-up, and improper swing technique place amateur golfers at greatest risk for injury. Correcting these deficiencies may result in fewer injuries—and more fun—on the golf course.

Let's turn now to look more closely at the golf swing and how repetition and technical errors in swing mechanics can lead to injury.

The Golf Swing and Injury

How does the golf swing contribute to golf-related injuries? In medical school, the first thing they teach you is anatomy. A firm grounding in anatomy is essential to understanding the disease process. In other words, you first must understand how things are *supposed* to be put together before you can figure out what's wrong. However, before we take a look at anatomy, which we will do in later chapters when we look at specific types of injuries, let's take a few minutes to look at the "anatomy," or phases, of the golf swing.

Phases of the Golf Swing

Golf instructors and golf medicine experts divide the swing into phases. Each phase of the golf swing (the address, the backswing, the downswing, impact, and follow-through) places

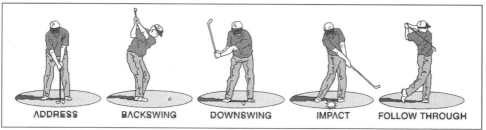

Figure 3-1. The phases of the golf swing. The golf swing can be divided into the address, backswing, downswing, impact, and follow-through phases.

15

demands on certain parts of the body and can result in specific types of injuries (7)(32).

Injuries to body tissues during the golf swing are caused by excessive tissue tension, twisting, or the stress absorbed by the golfer due to impact of the club with the ball, or, ground, or rock, or—whatever (7)(32).

The Address Phase

Figure 3-2. The address phase.

To properly prepare for the golf swing, you must first "address" the ball. This is the part of the golf swing where you tip your hat and in your best Ed Norton drawl say, "Hellooo ball." It works every time. The address is the least stressful golf swing phase (unless, of course, you happen to be playing with a big guy named Ralph).

During the address phase, body weight is evenly distributed on both feet, which should be roughly shoulder-width apart. The spine is tilted forward from the hips so that the spine is positioned at a right angle (90 degrees) to the club shaft. The knees are then relaxed (flexed) to center the body weight over the feet. The arms are extended and relaxed.

Please, I don't mean to offend the left-handed golfers reading this book, but the following discussion of swing mechanics, and the subsequent chapters focusing on specific injuries, are written from the perspective of the *right-handed* golfer. Thus, for our purposes, the *lead* side of the body (the side closest to the target) is the *left* side. This is important, because many common golf injuries (elbow and shoulder tendonitis, for example) occur primarily on the *leading* side. Lefties need to reverse the terms "left" and "right" in their mind as they read along.

The address is actually not particularly stressful in itself, but mistakes in grip or stance can lead to injury-causing consequences later in the swing.

The Backswing Phase

During the backswing, the club is raised to its highest point in the swing. Body weight is shifted to the right foot. Rotation of the hips, knees, shoulders, and spine occur, and the head remains relatively still. At the top of the backswing the left thumb, left wrist, and right wrist are in the cocked position, and the forearm muscles are stretched as far as they can.

Figure 3-3. The backswing phase.

Repetition and swing technique flaws during the backswing can lead to numerous problems, including wrist/thumb tendonitis, aggravation of wrist/thumb arthritis, wrist "impaction" syndrome, nerve stretch injuries of the wrist, elbow tendonitis (tennis elbow, golfer's elbow), shoulder impingement syndrome, and spine (especially lower-back) injury.

Less than one in four golf swing injuries are thought to occur during the backswing phase (69).

The Downswing Phase

During the downswing, the weight is shifted to the left foot while the knees, hips, and trunk rotate together to the left. A left-sided "uncoiling" occurs due to vigorous contraction of the

Figure 3-4. The downswing phase.

abdominal muscles (the muscles responsible for rotating the trunk) and the spinal muscles. The abdominal muscles are working three times harder during the downswing phase than during the backswing.

Similarly, the spinal muscles are working four to five times harder during the downswing, compared with the backswing. The right shoulder muscles (rotator cuff) and right pectoral muscles ("pecs") are also firing away. The pecs are now working six to seven times harder than they were during the backswing, in order to propel the club head (which accelerates to speeds of 100 miles per hour in about two-tenths of a second).

Repetition and swing technique flaws during the downswing can lead to numerous problems, including wrist tendonitis/strain, elbow tendonitis/strain, stress fractures of the ribs, and abdominal, pectoral, spinal, and shoulder muscle strain.

Injuries during the downswing are about twice as frequent as backswing injuries (69).

The Impact Phase

At Impact, the club makes contact with the ball—we hope. The wrists and hands complete the acceleration of the club head, the wrists unhinging in a whip-like motion as the right hand rotates over the left after the ball is hit. Body weight shifts to the left.

Figure 3-5. The impact phase.

The force of impact from hitting the ball (called the counterforce) is transmitted up the club to the body. If an object other than the ball is struck by the club head (for example, the ground, a tree, a rock), the counterforce is greatly increased.

Many muscles act together to keep the club head moving forward through the impact phase, effectively overcoming the counterforce. Without these hardworking muscles (which include the forearms and shoulder rotator cuff muscles), the club would screech to a halt at impact.

The majority of injuries related to the golf swing occur during the impact phase. Repetition and swing technique flaws during impact can lead to numerous problems, including wrist fracture (hamate bone), nerve compression injury (carpal tunnel syndrome), wrist/finger tendonitis (trigger finger), elbow tendonitis (tennis elbow, golfer's elbow), shoulder (rotator cuff) strain/tear, and aggravation of arthritis pain in the hip/knee.

The Follow-Through Phase

After striking the ball, the club gradually decelerates during the follow-through. The body rotates to the left around the spine. The wrists rotate about each other to create the "roll-over" motion of the hands. The hips and shoulders continue to rotate until the body is facing the target (or, in my case, my body is facing the water hazard). The spine hyperextends, and body weight completely shifts to the left side.

Figure 3-6. The follow-through phase. (Illustrations 3-1 through 3-6 by Moki Kokoris)

Repetition and swing technique flaws during the follow-through can lead to numerous problems, including spine hyperextension injury, knee sprain, ankle sprain, and hip bursitis/tendonitis.

About one in four golf swing injuries occur during the follow-through phase. Lower-back injuries are especially common (69).

Now that we have a basic understanding of golf swing mechanics, it's time to look at specific types of injuries. First, though, let's review, in the context of what we now know about swing mechanics, the main causes of golf injuries in the amateur. Injuries occur due to:

- *Poor physical conditioning.* The three components of physical conditioning are strength, flexibility, and aerobic fitness, and all three components are essential for the golfer to remain injury-free when extreme demands are placed on the body by the golf swing.

- *Overuse.* Even with a properly executed golf swing, trauma occurs to body tissues. These so-called "micro-trauma" injuries are usually no big deal—our bodies can usually repair the damage and be as good as new. However, with overpractice and excessive play, the rate of injury exceeds the body's capacity to heal, and chronic or even permanent painful injuries can result. Recall that overuse is a main contributing factor to injury among professional golfers.

- *Inadequate warm-up.* Studies show that there is a direct and positive relationship between the temperature of a muscle and that muscle's ability to do work. Specifically, a warmed-up muscle has more rapid electrical conduction, produces more force, is more energetically efficient, and is more flexible than a "cold" muscle. In short, a warmed-up muscle (or tendon) performs better and is less prone to injury than a cold muscle.

  How do muscles get warm? First, muscles are like little furnaces—they generate their own heat as they are used. Second, the increased blood flow delivered to our active muscles acts to warm them up even more (44). Swinging a golf club stresses the muscles and tendons to near full capacity. The importance of a proper warm-up routine before beginning play or practice cannot be overemphasized.

- *Poor swing technique.* We have already touched on how faulty swing mechanics can contribute to injury. Certainly, the amateur golfer is more prone to injuries due to poor swing mechanics than the professional. According to golf medicine experts Doctors Cornelius Stover and William Mallon, "lessons from a golf professional are probably the best method of developing proper technique to improve performance and decrease injury risk" (31). More swing pitfalls are noted in later chapters, in relation to specific injuries.

Now we can turn to some specific types of injuries our bodies might sustain while playing golf.

Strains, Sprains, Fractures, and Tendonitis in Golf

The vast majority of golf injuries are not the result of single traumatic or freak accidents. Rather, they occur as a result of tissue damage sustained over time from overuse and poor technique. Most golf injuries fall into the general categories of strains, sprains, fractures, and tendonitis. Because patients (and doctors) frequently use some of these terms interchangeably, it's important to be able to distinguish among them.

Strains

A *muscle strain* is a partial tearing or stretching injury to a muscle. If muscle fibers are overstretched, especially when they are vigorously contracting, they can tear. This usually results in immediate and severe pain in the involved muscle, in contrast to so-called "delayed-onset" muscle soreness, which sets in one to three days after strenuous muscle activity. (Delayed-onset muscle soreness does not reflect a serious muscle injury, and it usually resolves in a few days without treatment.)

The pain from a true muscle strain may be so great that the athlete cannot continue playing. The involved muscles (the quadriceps and hamstrings are commonly injured) will be tender to touch, swollen, black and blue (bruised), and painful to use. By the second day after injury, an intense local inflammatory reaction sets in. The intensity of the pain, swelling, and inflammation depends on how much muscle damage has occurred.

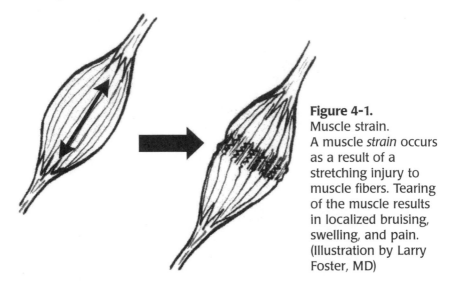

Figure 4-1.
Muscle strain.
A muscle *strain* occurs as a result of a stretching injury to muscle fibers. Tearing of the muscle results in localized bruising, swelling, and pain. (Illustration by Larry Foster, MD)

General guidelines for treatment of muscle strain injuries include:

- Rest, to limit pain and swelling and to prevent further injury to the damaged muscle. (Too much rest, however, is discouraged because it can lead to excessive muscle scarring and stiffness.)
- Ice, light compression (such as with an ACE-type bandage), and anti-inflammatory medication, for the first couple of days.
- A physical therapy program begun after the early (acute) phase of the injury has passed (a few days or so), helps restore normal muscle strength and flexibility.

Only after full muscle strength has been regained should a golfer return to play. Studies show that muscle fatigue and premature return to sports are both associated with muscle strain reinjury. Minor muscle strains can resolve pretty quickly (a week or so may do the trick), but a severe strain may take months to heal.

Muscle strains are best prevented by taking a few precautions. First, basic muscle fitness is important, as muscular strength and endurance are necessary to avoid injury. A strong and flexible muscle is less prone to injury than a weak, stiff, or fatigued muscle. Furthermore, proper muscle warm-up and stretching before play are important (50).

Sprains

A sprain is a stretching or tearing injury to a ligament (a specialized tissue that connects bone to bone). One common sprain injury occurring to the golfer is twisting an ankle when stepping in a rut on the course. Sprain injuries can be graded based on how severely the ligament tissue is damaged. A mild (low-grade) sprain involves a partial injury to the ligament, whereas a severe (high-grade) sprain results in a complete tear of the ligament and may require surgery to repair the ligament and restore joint stability. Sprain injuries are characterized by pain, swelling, tenderness, and limited joint motion.

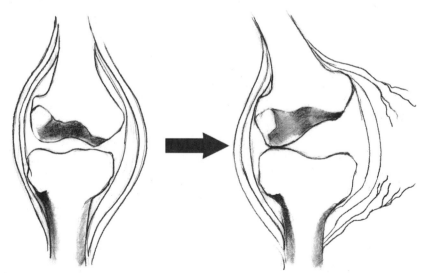

Figure 4-2. Ligament sprain. A *sprain* is a stretching or tearing injury to a ligament. Ligament tissue connects bone to bone and serves to stabilize joints. Stress applied to a joint can stretch the ligaments, resulting in partial or complete ligament tearing. Complete ligament tears result in joint instability and may require surgical repair. (Illustration by Suzanne AuBuchon)

Treatment for a ligament sprain is similar to treatment for a muscle strain:

- Rest, ice, light compression, elevation of the injured joint, and medication help control early swelling and pain.
- Early, gentle motion and avoidance of overimmobilization help minimize joint stiffness.
- In more serious cases, a physical therapy program is required to restore joint motion and strength before sports can safely be resumed.

It should come as no surprise that the strength of our ligaments decline as we age, making older golfers more prone to sprain injuries (23).

Fractures

A fracture is a failure of bone tissue. Excessive compression, twisting (torsion), or bending forces cause bones to fracture. Although fractures are relatively rare in the game of golf, slip-and-fall-type of fractures can happen on the golf course just as they can in your own backyard.

To an orthopedic surgeon, the terms *fracture* and *break* are interchangeable. But it's not surprising that time and time again I encounter patients who are convinced that a fracture is more serious than a break.

"I'm sorry to tell you this, Mr. Jones, but your metatarsal bone is broken."

"Whew! That's all? I was afraid you were going to say it's *fractured!*"

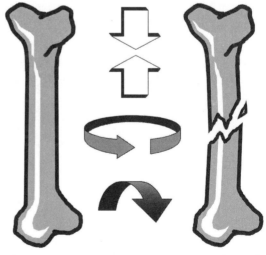

Figure 4-3. Bone fracture. A *fracture* (break) is a failure of bone tissue due to excessive compression, twisting, or bending. (Illustration by Moki Kokoris)

But perhaps even more surprising is that just as many patients are convinced that a break is *worse* than a fracture! Sometimes I ask patients which they think is worse. I have to laugh a little when they look at me like I have two heads and say, "Gee, Doc, you mean you don't know the difference between a break and a fracture? Where did *you* go to medical school?"

A *stress fracture* occurs when bone is injured by repeated small stresses (micro-trauma) rather than one big catastrophic crunch. In golf, stress fractures have been reported to occur in the wrist and the ribs. In many cases of stress fracture, X-rays may appear to be normal. This can make diagnosing a stress fracture tricky at times.

Tendonitis

A great many golf-related injuries involve tendons, so I shall describe tendon anatomy, injury, and treatment in some detail.

In the practice of medicine, the questions that seem most simple can be the most difficult to answer. "What is tendonitis?" is very common, and I'm never really quite sure how to answer. On one level, the simple response is that tendonitis involves inflammation ("itis") of a tendon—any structure that connects muscle to bone.

"Duh," I can hear my patients thinking. "It took you how many years of doctor school to come up with *that?*"

The truth is that even experts can't agree on exactly what tendonitis is.

Tendons are very specialized tissues designed to connect muscles (which do the work) to bones (which support us and help us move around). Our muscles have cells that can contract (shorten). Tendons act as the go-betweens, connecting the muscles to the bones. At one end of the tendon a blending with muscle tissue occurs; at the other end, the tendon firmly anchors into the bone.

Tendons are designed to withstand immense stretching (tensile) stresses. Think of tendons as biological "ropes." Like conventional ropes, tendons are composed of many tiny parallel fibers. These fibers are made up primarily of a tough protein called collagen. Bone and numerous other body tissues, including cartilage and ligaments, are also made up largely of collagen. The bulk of tendon tissue is composed of collagen and water, with only a few living cells (called fibroblasts) scattered about (23).

This combination of a resilient, multicord tendon and a firm bone anchor allows our tendons to absorb and transmit huge stretching loads. The thicker the tendon (that is, the greater its cross-sectional area), the stronger it is. In fact, the strength of a tendon is estimated to be more than twice the strength of its corresponding muscle (23).

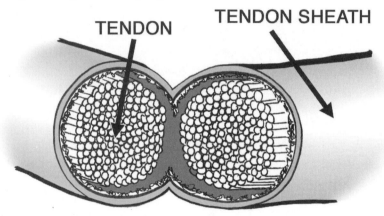

Figure 4-4. Basic tendon anatomy. Tendons, like ropes, are made up of numerous tiny parallel fibers. The bulk of tendon tissue is made up of these fibers and water. Many tendons are surrounded by a *sheath* that provides the tendon with nourishment and lubrication. (Illustration by Larry Foster, MD)

Tendons can be injured by any one of several mechanisms. Cutting (laceration) of a tendon, while common overall, does not occur in golf (though my golfing buddy Brian has a slice that could cut a tomato). Direct blows that cause contusions can also injure a tendon. But the most common mechanism of tendon injury in golf—and in life—involves simply pulling too hard on the tendon.

When a stretching load on a tendon exceeds the tendon's mechanical strength, tendon failure occurs. Sometimes, a load suddenly and greatly exceeds the tendon's strength, resulting in catastrophic and complete tendon failure. Such a failure might occur when a tennis player lunges for a shot and ruptures her Achilles tendon.

More often, however, tendons sustain only partial (perhaps even microscopic) tears. These subtle injuries occur not as the result of a single gross overload but as a cumulative effect of smaller but repeated tendon stresses. Just how many balls *were* there in that super-jumbo bucket you hit at the range last Sunday?

It is usually these low-magnitude but high-repetition tendon injuries that give us the "itis" in tendonitis. Unfortunately, tendons have a couple of strikes against them when it comes to their ability to repair and heal themselves. First, in tendon tissue there are relatively few living cells available to perform the actual repair work. Second, tendons in general have a paltry blood supply, so the raw materials needed for repair (oxygen, nutrients, and so on) are in short supply.

Tendonitis, then, is a reflection both of tendon injury and of the body's often slow healing process for tendons. It is characterized by localized swelling, tenderness to touch, and pain when the injured tendon is further stressed. Individuals who are at high risk for developing tendonitis in an upper limb include people who habitually place repeated stress on their tendons, such as assembly-line workers, fishermen, craftsmen, and athletes, such as tennis players and—you guessed it—golfers (9)(13).

Treatment for tendonitis is similar to treatment for strain and sprain injuries:

- Rest is the recommended initial treatment.
- Immobilization. Depending on how acute and severe the symptoms are, a short period of strict immobilization (splinting or casting, for example) may be prescribed. However, too much rest for an injured tendon can lead to joint stiffness and muscle shrinkage/weakness (atrophy). Therefore, when your doctor tells you to *rest*, it most likely means that you should identify and elimi-

nate, or at least minimize, the activities that are causing the problem. (It's probably going to take more than merely switching to a mini-jumbo bucket of balls at the driving range.)

- Ice and medication. Ice and anti-inflammatory medication can also help lessen the pain and swelling of acute tendonitis.

The Role of Physical Therapy

While it is true that many mild sprain, strain, and tendonitis injuries will resolve on their own with a little rest and time, injuries that become chronic may require more formal and supervised treatment. Physical therapy is a mainstay of treatment for many chronic overuse injuries sustained in golf, such as tendonitis. To rehabilitate an injured golfer, the therapist takes a step-wise approach.

The initial goal is to focus both on reducing pain and inflammation and on retaining joint range of motion. Only when that goal has been reached does the therapist begin a sport-specific progressive exercise program designed to maximize strength and endurance by enhancing the healing process and restoring strength to the injured tendons, muscles, and joints.

Some of the most commonly used tools and methods therapists have at their disposal are:

- Cold therapy (cryotherapy) is typically used in the acute (early) stages of treatment. Ice, cold packs, and cold whirlpools can all be helpful. Ice, nature's own anti-inflammatory, can be applied at home or in the clubhouse for up to twenty minutes at a time. Ice helps deaden pain and control local swelling after an injury (58). However, excessive use of cold or ice treatment can actually lead to an *increase* in swelling (50).

- Cold therapy is also employed in the treatment of some chronic muscular injuries, particularly in the case of "trigger points" of the neck and lower back. Here, the injured muscle and tendon are treated with a topical cooling spray (such as fluoromethane) followed by a manual stretching of the muscle. This "spray and stretch" technique is believed to increase the mobility of the injured muscle, increase range of motion, and decrease pain (28)(45).

- Heat therapy, typically used after the acute phase of injury and inflammation has passed, is applied to increase blood flow to the tissues, improve muscle and tendon flexibility, decrease pain, and promote healing. Heat lamps, a hot whirlpool, and paraffin can be used to deliver heat energy to the skin and superficial tissues. Ultrasound machines utilize a skin surface transducer and coupling gel to transmit pulses of sound energy to selected *deep* tissues. When these deep tissues (muscle, bone, ligaments) absorb the ultrasound energy, the energy is converted to heat. Ultrasound is often used by therapists to "warm up" tissues (literally) before undergoing a session of stretching and exercises (28)(45).

- Phonophoresis is a technique that combines ultrasound and a steroid-based skin cream.

- Electrical stimulation is used in various ways to treat both acute and chronic golf injuries. Transcutaneous electrical nerve stimulation (TENS) helps reduce pain by blocking the body's production of chemical pain messengers. Portable battery-powered units are now available. Electrical stimulation can also be used to control swelling and stimulate muscle contraction to prevent muscle atrophy (45). (Collectively, the use of heat, cold, electrical stimulation, ultrasound, and so on, are referred to as therapy "modalities.")

- Massage (both superficial and deep) in various forms is used to control pain and promote healing.

- Range of motion (ROM) exercises are employed by the therapist to progressively move a joint, with the goal of restoring full joint motion. ROM exercises can be passive, active, or active-assistive. With passive ROM, the therapist manipulates and stretches the joint without the aid of the patient's muscles. Active-assistive ROM occurs when the patient's joint is mobilized by a combination of his own muscles and the assistance of the therapist. With active ROM the patient is in complete control of the joint movement and using only his own muscles.

- Strengthening exercises provide resistance to the muscles. Physical training increases the cross-sectional area of muscle fibers, resulting in an increase in muscle bulk and strength (44).

As the science of sports medicine becomes more sophisticated, so does the science of sports injury rehabilitation. A proper rehabilitation program should be tailored to the particular athlete. You would not want to rehabilitate an injured weightlifter with the same regimen used for an injured golfer. In fact, you would not want to rehabilitate a twenty-five-year-old golfer with the same regimen used for a seventy-two-year-old golfer.

Recently, the concept of the Interval Sports Program (ISP) has been proposed. These programs are designed by doctors and therapists to gradually rehabilitate injured structures in a *stepwise* manner that is *sport-specific*. For instance, separate treatment protocols exist for baseball, tennis, and golf.

Here are some principles and guidelines of Interval Sports Programs (57):

- Before beginning the program, a patient must demonstrate full joint range of motion, minimal discomfort, and adequate muscle strength/endurance to be ready to resume sports activities.
- The program focuses on the entire body, with a gradual progression of sports activities and adopting proper body mechanics and warm-up habits to reduce the risk of reinjury.
- The program is individually tailored to the skills, goals, and injury of each patient.
- The program's activities are supplemented with an exercise program on alternate days.

A sample five-week ISP for the golfer rehabilitating from an injury or surgery might include:

- Week 1: Putting and chipping
- Week 2: Chipping and short irons
- Week 3: Short/medium irons
- Week 4: Long irons and driving
- Week 5: Full play (nine holes, then eighteen at end of week)

By gradually increasing the type, intensity, and number of golf shots, and by supplementing golf activities with stretching and strengthening exercises, the Interval Sports Program ultimately restores the golfer to full competition status (57).

If you are serious about golf—and if you are serious about not being *re-injured* the first time you return to the golf course— you owe it to yourself to make sure you are not being treated on an assembly-line basis. That is to say, the value of a well-trained and attentive physical therapist cannot be overstated.

Therapists are an integral part of the medical team. While treating you for a particular condition (elbow tendonitis, let's say), your doctor may see you on three or four occasions. Your therapist, on the other hand, is likely to be treating you several times a week for a couple of months.

Once therapy has returned the golfer to good health, play on the course can safely resume. But remember: if mechanical flaws in the golf swing contributed to the original injury, the player needs to correct that problem too. Otherwise, despite appropriate rehabilitation, a disappointing re-injury will likely occur. This is where a consultation with a local golf pro is essential.

Medication

Orthopedists frequently prescribe nonsteroidal anti-inflammatory drugs (NSAIDs) for patients suffering from strains, sprains, and tendonitis. The dozens of such products available are all basically chemical cousins of aspirin (the granddaddy of all NSAIDs). These drugs act to block the body's production of certain chemicals that cause inflammation.

Anti-inflammatory medications have not been shown to speed up the healing process, though. They just make the trip a little easier to take. They help lessen pain, and they may take the edge off enough to allow a person to continue sports. (I've been known to take NSAIDs so my bum back doesn't interfere too much with my golfing fun.)

As with any medication, side effects are possible. Interactions with other medications, stomach upset and bleeding, and kidney problems can occur. Make sure you check with your doctor and pharmacist before using any NSAID. As for which brand is best, I really can't say. Some of the older NSAIDs, such as aspirin and ibuprofen, are available inexpensively over the counter and work just fine. Some newer NSAIDs, such as the "Cox-2" inhibitors, are more convenient to take (only once a day) and are touted to have fewer side effects, but they are substantially more expensive and are available by prescription only.

Cortisone

Cortisone is a steroid-based medication that, for tendonitis, is injected into and around the zone of inflamed tissue. (And no, the needle does not go into the bone, as many patients fear.) The steroid blocks the body's local inflammatory response by interfering with the formation of certain body chemicals that are necessary for inflammation to occur.

Cortisone is a particularly useful tool for the physician in the treatment of tendonitis. It is routinely used as an aid in treating several tendonitis conditions common to golfers—tennis elbow, golfer's elbow, and shoulder tendonitis. As with any treatment, there are both good and not-so-good aspects associated with the use of cortisone.

The benefit of cortisone is that it can provide dramatic pain relief within a couple of days after the injection, with little risk of serious side effects. I have seen many patients with painful tendonitis get welcome relief from a simple injection given in the office.

However, cortisone is *not* always a cure for tendonitis. One study of the use of cortisone in treatment of elbow tendonitis found that nearly 90 percent of patients who received an injection reported pain relief, but up to half those patients went on to have recurrent pain (11). Another recently published study found that, while patients who received a cortisone injection for elbow tendonitis did get some early pain relief, the long-term outcome was no different than the outcome with patients who received a placebo injection (49). It is important to note also that *repeated* local cortisone injection has been linked to delayed tendon healing, tendon degeneration, and tendon rupture. In practice, I usually limit the use of cortisone.

The occasional local cortisone injection does not carry with it the serious health risks associated with oral or intravenous steroid medication. I do have one story, though. One day, a female patient returned to the office about a month after receiving a cortisone injection.

"Doctor," she said, "are there any side effects to the steroid injection you gave me?"

I asked her why she wanted to know. She then unbuttoned the top button of her blouse, revealing a thick mat of hair on her chest.

I was shocked and asked, "Holy smoke, how far down does that hair go?"

She replied, "All the way down to my *nuts!*"

(Come on, it's just a joke!)

So, although we do have effective methods of treating the strains, sprains, and tendonitis injuries associated with golf, the road to recovery can be frustratingly slow—especially when you're sitting on the sideline nursing an injury while your buddies play without you. Your grandmother gave the best advice: An ounce of prevention is worth a pound of cure.

The best way to prevent musculoskeletal injury during golf is to combine basic physical conditioning, proper preplay stretching and warm-up, appropriate equipment selection, and sound swing mechanics—with a little good luck thrown in.

Certainly, there are many other golf-related injuries and health conditions I could cover—heat exhaustion, lightning injuries, the ravages of toe fungus, and on and on. But I've decided to stick to orthopedic injuries because I know a little bit about them, and because they interest me the most. I do want to tell one interesting story, though, about a nonorthopedic golf injury I once saw.

When I was a medical student at Columbia University, I had the chance to work in the emergency room of a suburban New Jersey hospital for one summer. One day, a woman brought in her husband unconscious and bleeding from the head.

"Help us!" she pleaded. "I was playing golf with my husband, and I hit him on the back of the head with a golf ball."

We rushed the man to the treatment room, where we struggled for an hour to revive him, to no avail. I had to break the news to the sweet old lady.

"I'm sorry to tell you this, Mrs. Shankman, but your husband is gone."

As she cried, I had to ask her, "Tell me, why were there *two* ball marks on the back of your husband's head?"

"Well," she sniffed, "the second one was my Mulligan."

Now that we've covered the general types of injuries golf can cause, let's turn now to distinct injuries to specific body parts. The next several chapters spotlight injuries to the elbow, wrist and hand, back and spine, shoulder, and knee.

Elbow Injuries

Joe is a friend of mine. I hate Joe. Well, let's just say I'm extremely jealous of him. He has two jobs (firefighter and insurance agent), he coaches about six different Little League teams simultaneously, and he still manages to play three or four rounds of golf a week and shoots in the low 80s. I don't know how he does it!

A couple of years ago, Joe came to me complaining of elbow pain.

"Doc, I don't know what I did, but my elbow is killing me. It's getting serious—I can't swing a club."

He rubbed the outer part of his left elbow and performed an imaginary golf swing to make the point. I *do* hate him. Even his *imaginary* swings look better than mine!

Even though it was the dead of winter in New York, Joe had been at the local indoor driving range getting ready for the first hint of warm weather, pounding away at countless buckets of balls. At first, the elbow bothered him only when he hit the ball. Then he began feeling pain when lifting his coffee cup, opening the garage door, and squeezing the toothpaste tube. The thought of running into a burning building didn't bother the firefighter Joe at all, but the thought of missing a few months of golf because of a sore elbow—now *that* was scary.

From time to time, all of us have thoughts that we're ashamed of peep out briefly from our subconscious. (Does pushing your boss in front of an oncoming locomotive sound familiar?) For one millisecond, I found myself thinking, "Serves him right." Then I remembered that pesky Hippocratic Oath I took, and decided to help him out.

Surveys of both professional and amateur golfers have shown that the elbow is a common site of injury. The elbow accounts for about 10 percent of injuries among the professionals. For the amateur, the elbow accounts for about one in three golf-related injuries (29), and the vast majority of elbow injuries (for both amateur and pro) are tendon injuries.

Several factors have been identified as risk factors for elbow injuries in golf:

- Advancing age
- Faulty swing mechanics
- Lack of conditioning
- Insufficient warm-up
- Excessive play or practice

For golfers age thirty-five to fifty-five, studies show that playing more than two rounds a week is likely to increase the risk of elbow injury (29). Advancing age is the only risk factor we golfers don't have at least some degree of control over. People ask me if I'm upset about recently reaching the Big 4-0. Well, I guess I'm not too thrilled, but it sure beats the heck out of the alternative. So far, the worst thing is my sudden preference for relaxed-fit jeans.

Earlier in the book, we discussed the relationship between overuse, tendon injury, and the development of tendonitis. Now we turn to elbow tendonitis and the role of swing mechanics, as well as some dos and don'ts from the experts. First, let's start with some basic anatomy.

Elbow Anatomy 101

The elbow is composed of three bones: the *humerus* (the bone in the upper arm) and the *radius* and the *ulna* in the forearm.

A fancy hinge joint that can not only swing back and forth (flex and extend) but also swivel, the elbow allows the forearm and the hand to rotate into the palm-down position (pronation) and the palm-up position (supination). All these motions come into play during the golf swing.

Many muscles act together to control motion at this elbow joint. The main elbow flexor muscles are the brachialis and the biceps (the "Popeye" muscle). The action of the triceps muscle in the back of the upper arm plays a main role in extending (straightening) the elbow.

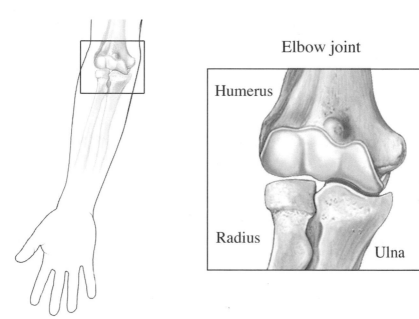

Elbow joint

Humerus

Radius

Ulna

Figure 5-1. Basic elbow anatomy. The elbow is composed of three bones: the *humerus* (the bone in the upper arm), and the *radius* and the *ulna* in the forearm. The elbow is a fancy hinge joint that can flex/extend, and swivel. (Copyright 2003 Nucleus Medical Art, all rights reserved. www.nucleusinc.com)

Elbow Tendonitis:
Tennis Elbow and Golfer's Elbow

Among golfers, the elbow is the most common site of tendonitis. The most frequent form of elbow tendonitis in golf involves injury to the outer (lateral) side of the elbow and is commonly referred to as *tennis elbow.* (That's what my friend Joe had.) Tendonitis localized to the inner (medial) side of the elbow occurs less frequently and is called *golfer's elbow.*

What? Golfers get tennis elbow? Patients' immediate response to the diagnosis of tennis elbow is, of course, "Gee, Doc. I don't even *play* tennis!" Confusing, I know! So let me clarify right away:

- Anyone can get tennis elbow—not just tennis players.
- Anyone can get golfer's elbow—not just golfers.
- Golfers get tennis elbow *more frequently* than they get golfer's elbow.

Still with me? The whole thing would have been simpler if the doctor who first discovered these conditions had been a golf nut instead of a tennis buff!

Actually, tennis elbow and golfer's elbow frequently are not caused by sports at all. Any recreational or occupational activity that places repeated stresses on the wrist, elbow, or forearm can result in elbow tendonitis. For example, meat-cutters, plumbers, and weavers have all been identified as being at higher risk for developing elbow tendonitis (8).

I don't play much tennis—I'm quite partial to golf, in case you hadn't guessed—and I don't like the term "tennis elbow" for golf injuries, for obvious reasons. Plus, I didn't hurt my elbow by prancing around in white shorts waving a racquet at a fuzzy ball. Heck no. I hurt my elbow by smashing a rock-hard projectile back and forth and back and forth across thousands of yards of open land, tearing up huge clods of earth along the way.

I guess things could be worse, though. Imagine your golfing buddy coming up to you after nine holes and saying, "Sorry, Bill, I can't play the back nine today. My weaver's elbow is just killing me!"

Tennis Elbow (Lateral Epicondylitis)

Many muscles in the forearm act to straighten the wrist and fingers—for simplicity's sake, let's call these muscles the *extensors*. The tendons of these muscles converge and meld together to form a structure called the *common extensor tendon*. This common tendon, in turn, anchors into a small bony ridge on the outer portion of the elbow called the *lateral epicondyle* of the humerus.

Now, that's where we run into trouble. Imagine a steamship that pulls up to a dock and has all its ropes tied to only a single cleat on the wharf. In calm weather, things would probably be okay, but if a gust of wind should come, the collective tugging of all those ropes concentrated on that single cleat might well yank

Figure 5-2. Doctor Divot's steamship analogy of elbow tendonitis. At the elbow, the tendons of several strong extensor muscles meld together and insert on the bone at a single anchor spot. Like a ship that has all its ropes tied to one dock cleat, this results in very high stresses concentrated in a small area and can lead to injury where the tendons anchor to the bone. (Illustration by Larry Foster MD)

the cleat loose from where it is bolted to the dock. We can apply this steamship analogy to the extensor tendons, which are like the ropes—all of them pulling on one anchor spot (the lateral epicondyle, the cleat).

The extensor muscles are quite active in tennis players. They are responsible for keeping the wrist rigid for a backhand shot. In golf, the *right* extensors stabilize the right wrist when initiating the backswing. The *left* extensors are most active at the impact phase of the swing, keeping the left wrist rigid as contact is made with the ball (8)(13). Tennis elbow can occur when excessive stress leads to microscopic injury and tearing of the common extensor tendon fibers where they anchor into the bone, at the lateral epicondyle.

Tennis elbow occurs more frequently in the left (lead) elbow because the left extensor tendons encounter more strain during the swing than the right extensors. With each swing, microscopic stressing of the extensor tendons occurs. Hitting the ground or another object during the swing greatly increases the stress on the left elbow extensors.

Just as in the steamship analogy—where a sudden gust of wind pushes the ship away from the wharf, and the ropes are yanked tight—so too during the golf swing a sudden burst of muscle activity generates huge stresses on the extensor tendons. Repeated pulling of the rope on the cleat will eventually lead to its gradual loosening from the dock. To some extent, our bodies are able to repair the day-to-day damage before permanent injury sets in—sort of like a dock master who comes around every day and tightens the bolts on the cleat. However, repeated tendon injury that exceeds the body's capacity for repair can result in the formation of painful scar tissue—tennis elbow (8)(11).

Most frequently, common extensor tendon injury occurs as a result of repeated stressing over time. Thus, most patients who come to me with tennis elbow note a *gradual* onset of elbow pain. Few can recall a specific moment in time when the elbow suddenly began to hurt. Most of my patients have symptoms for weeks or months before they seek medical treatment.

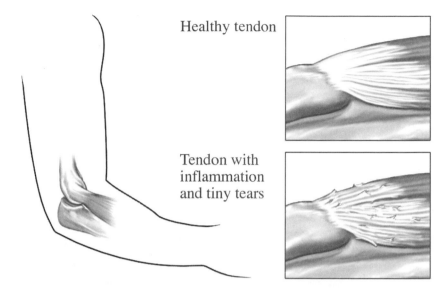

Healthy tendon

Tendon with
inflammation
and tiny tears

Figure 5-3. Tennis elbow (lateral epicondylitis). Tennis elbow occurs when excessive stress leads to microscopic tears and inflammation where the common extensor tendon fibers anchor into the bone (right elbow is shown here). (Copyright 2003 Nucleus Medical Art, all rights reserved. www.nucleusinc.com)

Evaluating a patient for tennis elbow:
- Pain is the main symptom. The pain is centered at the outer elbow (the lateral epicondyle) and can radiate into the forearm.
- The pain is usually accentuated by any activity requiring wrist extension, such as hitting a golf shot, but also lifting a suitcase, shaking hands, holding a coffee pot, and so on.
- On physical exam, there is a tender "hot spot" localized over the outer elbow.
- Patients complain of pain and weakness when asked to squeeze the physician's fingers or when asked to perform the "chair test" (lifting a light chair a couple inches into the air by grasping the chair back palm-down and lifting straight up).

- Elbow range of motion is usually normal, though many patients complain of elbow stiffness.
- Numbness and tingling are absent.
- X-rays of the elbow typically are normal but may occasionally reveal calcifications at the site of the tendonitis (8)(11).

By taking a careful history and performing a physical examination, your doctor can rule out other clinical problems that can mimic some of the symptoms of tennis elbow, such as elbow arthritis, elbow ligament injury, and various forms of pinched nerves in the forearm or neck (8)(11).

Once tennis elbow has been diagnosed, a treatment plan can be drawn up. The first thing I tell patients is that tennis elbow is a difficult condition to get rid of and that it may take months before their pain resolves. Then I emphasize that I have no single magic-bullet cure for tennis elbow, and that successful treatment usually is the result of a combination of several treatment strategies—that is, more of a shotgun approach than a magic bullet.

Treatment for tennis elbow can include a combination of strategies (8)(11):

- Rest. The goal of the initial phase of tennis elbow treatment is to calm down the acute pain and inflammation, which can be quite severe. First, the patient needs to identify and avoid activities that aggravate the symptoms. On the surface, this seems like a no-brainer, but let's see *you* try to convince some golf nut that he'd be better off postponing his long-awaited trip to Myrtle Beach! Complete inactivity and too much elbow immobilization are, I believe, counterproductive. I encourage my patients to keep their elbows moving even though they may be sore.
- Pain relief. Nonsteroidal anti-inflammatory drugs (NSAIDs) can help take the edge off the pain.
- Physical therapy. Once the acutely painful phase of tennis elbow is under control, the rehabilitation phase of treatment can begin. I routinely refer my patients with

tennis elbow for physical therapy. In recent years, more emphasis has been placed on rehabilitative exercise for the treatment of many forms of tendonitis, including tennis elbow. The basic premise is that a strengthened (rehabilitated) muscle and tendon are subject to less stress and injury (13).

Initially, the therapist focuses on regaining elbow motion by means of progressive stretching exercises, and on treating inflammation with the various modalities, such as ultrasound, electrical stimulation, and iontophoresis. (A recently published study found that extracorporeal shock-wave treatment, using the same technology employed to zap kidney stones, is of no benefit in the treatment of tennis elbow [52].)

Then the therapist introduces a progressively intensive muscle-strengthening program complemented by a home stretching/exercise program.

- Bracing. "Counterforce" braces have many design variations, but most are worn as forearm straps designed to apply pressure (counterforce) to the extensor muscles just downstream from the tender lateral epicondyle. The theory is that the brace takes some of the stress away from the injured tendon attachment site. Many people feel these braces help, especially when worn during sports or other strenuous activities. However, it is not scientifically clear why, or even if, these devices work (9)(11). As long as my patients do not view these braces as a substitute for rehab, I do not discourage their use.

- Cortisone. The steroid-based cortisone medication is injected around the tender lateral epicondyle, to block the body's local inflammatory response. Within a few days, the cortisone kicks in and the resulting pain relief can be substantial. The percentage of patients reporting pain relief after a cortisone injection has been reported to approach 90 percent, but in about half these patients the pain recurs (11). However, the honeymoon period of pain relief after an injection can be a double-edged sword: patients may think they are cured and be apt to forget about all the other important elements of their treatment, such as rest and therapy. So, while cortisone can be a useful aid in the treatment of many kinds of tendonitis, it is rarely a magic-bullet cure.

(One recent study has concluded that, aside from providing some early pain relief, cortisone provided no significant benefit and that rehabilitation should be the first line of treatment for tennis elbow in patients with a short duration of symptoms [49]).

Once pain relief, strength, flexibility, and endurance have been optimized, sports can safely resume. It takes a big commitment of time—sometimes several months—and patience to treat tennis elbow successfully. I encourage my patients to hang in there, that if they want to make an omelet they have to be willing to crack some eggs. Nonsurgical treatment of tennis elbow, when properly performed, has a success rate of about 90 percent.

However, the lessons and habits learned during treatment must not be forgotten once the patient returns to the golf course, or a disappointing relapse can occur. Most of the tennis elbow patients who suffer from recurrent symptoms do so because of *incomplete rehabilitation* or *discontinuing preventative measures prematurely* (11). In addition, lessons from a golf pro can help eliminate swing flaws that may cause re-injury.

Because of its good track record, nonsurgical treatment of tennis elbow is usually the first choice. Patients who do not get satisfactory relief from nonsurgical approaches are then considered for surgery. There is no hard-and-fast rule about which patients should be offered surgery, but those with continued pain despite six to twelve months of well-managed nonsurgical treatment are generally considered to be candidates for surgery (8)(11).

When I was still in training, one of my professors told me that all orthopedic surgical procedures have one of two purposes—to take scar tissue away, or to make scar tissue where it is needed. Well, the surgery for tennis elbow does both. First, the scarred portion of the chronically injured common extensor tendon tissue is identified and removed, then the remaining tendon is reattached to the bone. New, and hopefully painless, scar tissue forms to secure that reattachment. After surgery, a rehab program is prescribed to regain motion and strength.

Tennis elbow surgery generally has good results. About 90 percent of patients have excellent pain relief and can resume full activities. About 10 percent will have some, but not complete, pain relief. Another 2 or 3 percent of surgical patients will not see any improvement in their pain (8)(11). Patients who return to sports, including golf, do so about six to twelve months after surgery.

Golfer's Elbow (Medial Epicondylitis)

Golfer's elbow in many ways plays second fiddle to the more talked-about and common tennis elbow, yet the two conditions have much in common. Golfer's elbow and tennis elbow develop for the same reasons, and treatment for both conditions is similar.

About five to ten times less common than tennis elbow, golfer's elbow is seen not only in golfers but also in tennis players, rowers, bowlers, archers, and baseball players (especially pitchers). Certain occupational stresses, such as typing, hammering, and repetitive use of a screwdriver are also risk factors for developing golfer's elbow (8)(11).

Golfer's elbow causes symptoms on the inner (medial) side of the elbow. The group of strong muscles located on the inner half of the forearm—we shall call them the *flexors*—is responsible for the flexing of the wrist and fingers. The tendons from these muscles blend together to form a *common flexor tendon*, which then anchors into a small ridge of bone on the inner side of the elbow called the *medial epicondyle* of the humerus.

If this all sounds familiar, it's because I described the same concept in relation to tennis elbow. In both tennis and golfer's elbow, several strong muscles merge to form a common tendon that then anchors into a small area of bone. The steamship analogy I used for tennis elbow applies here for golfer's elbow as well—too many ropes yanking on one cleat.

The flexor muscles in the right forearm are responsible for stabilizing the wrist at the *impact* phase of the swing. Research has demonstrated that there is a burst of flexor muscle activity at the moment of impact with the ball. At the point of contact, these muscles are estimated to be contracting at up to 90 percent of their maximum capacity (9). That only a 10 percent reserve of muscle capacity remains during a golf swing is testimony to the fact that the golf swing is a stressful sports activity. (Lucky for me! Otherwise I'd be writing a diet book, or something.)

Golfer's elbow occurs as repeated tendon stressing leads to microscopic tearing and trauma to the common flexor tendon at its bony insertion site, resulting in degeneration, inflammation, and scar formation. Improper sports technique, poor muscle conditioning, and inadequate warm-up before sports activity are all believed to contribute to injury to the common flexor tendon (8)(11). As with tennis elbow, most patients with golfer's elbow notice a *gradual* onset of pain rather than sudden pain associated with a specific injury.

Evaluating a patient for golfer's elbow:

- Pain is the main symptom. The discomfort is centered at the inner elbow (the medial epicondyle) and can radiate into the forearm.
- Activities that stress the flexor muscles and tendons, such as hitting a forehand shot in tennis, throwing a ball, or hitting a golf shot, accentuate the pain. Golfer's elbow will typically cause the golfer pain in the right inner elbow when impact with the ball is made.
- On physical exam, there is a tender "hot spot" localized over the inner elbow.
- Patients note pain and weakness with squeezing, grasping, or lifting an object with the palm facing up.
- Elbow range of motion is usually normal, though many patients complain of elbow stiffness.

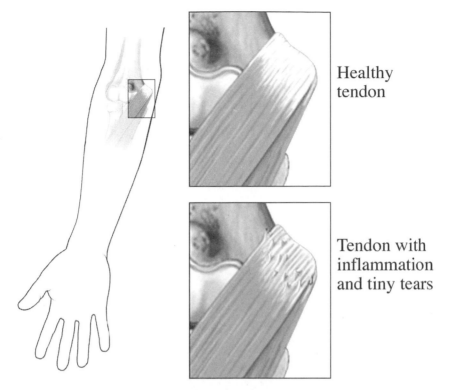

Healthy
tendon

Tendon with
inflammation
and tiny tears

Figure 5-4. Golfer's elbow (medial epicondylitis). Golfer's elbow occurs when excessive stress leads to microscopic tears and inflammation where the common flexor tendon fibers anchor into the bone (right elbow is shown here). (Copyright 2003 Nucleus Medical Art, all rights reserved. www.nucleusinc.com)

- X-rays of the elbow are usually normal but may reveal calcifications at the site of the tendonitis.
- Unlike tennis elbow, golfer's elbow can be associated with neurological symptoms: numbness and tingling into the ring and pinky fingers. This is true because the ulnar nerve lies just behind the medial epicondyle, so the nerve can become irritated along with the common flexor tendon. It's your ulnar nerve that gives you that zinging "funny bone" feeling in your forearm and pinky when you bang your inner elbow. Far be it from me to second-guess the Almighty, but putting the ulnar nerve right there—exposed and unprotected—is a pretty glaring design flaw.

(Okay, so he made up for it when he came up with beer and pizza.)

Taking a good history and performing a thorough physical exam will allow your doctor to confidently diagnose golfer's elbow and rule out other common causes of inner elbow pain, such as elbow arthritis or ligament injury. At that point, treatment can begin.

As with tennis elbow, treatment for golfer's elbow usually includes a combination of rest, activity modification, medication, and rehab.

- Rest helps give the body an opportunity to recover from golfer's elbow. Injured muscles and tendons are more susceptible to fatigue and further injury, and rest helps to break the cycle.

- NSAID medication can help the symptoms of pain and discomfort.

- Cortisone, used sparingly, can be helpful—but it is rarely the magic-bullet cure patients often hope for.

- Physical therapy/rehabilitation is a cornerstone of successful treatment. Various modalities, such as ultrasound, electrical stimulation, and iontophoresis, may be used for pain control, followed by a progressive stretching and strengthening of the flexor muscles and tendons.

- Six to ten weeks of therapy is not uncommon. The final stage of treatment is a sport-specific exercise program followed by a gradual return to sports (8)(9)(11).

The great majority of patients with golfer's elbow will get better nonsurgically. If a patient fails to obtain satisfactory pain relief after a *conscientiously* applied program of nonsurgical treatment, then surgery can be considered. Several authors recommend a trial of at least six to twelve months of nonoperative treatment before resorting to surgery(8)(11).

Most surgical procedures for golfer's elbow focus on identifying and removing the scarred portion of the common flexor tendon. The remaining normal tissue is then allowed to heal back to the bone. If needed, surgery can also be performed at the same time, through the same incision, to reduce irritation and pressure on the ulnar nerve. After surgery, the patient is placed back into therapy to regain range of motion and strength. Total recovery usually takes several months, and a return to golf and other sports may take up to one year.

Elbow Tendonitis and the Golf Swing

The golf swing is tough on the forearm flexor and extensor tendons. First, these muscles are firing at near full capacity in order to control the club head at various phases of the swing.

Figure 5-5. Elbow tendonitis and the golf swing. The elbow is susceptible to tendonitis injuries (tennis elbow and golfer's elbow) at the *transition* from the backswing to the downswing (left image). Vigorous muscle contraction and tendon stretching from excessive wrist motion can lead to elbow tendonitis. At *impact* (right image), the flexor and extensor muscles and tendons are also under added stress as they absorb the force of the impact with the ball. An even greater jolt is absorbed by the elbows if the club strikes the ground or an object. (Illustration by Moki Kokoris)

Second, the common flexor and extensor tendons are stretched when the wrist is flexed and extended during the golf swing. With the contracting muscles already under strain, any *excessive* wrist flexion/extension, due to poor swing mechanics, increases the risk of developing elbow tendonitis. In addition, at the moment of impact the elbows absorb an extra jolt from the ball, and an even bigger jolt if the golfer hits the ground or another object. Therefore, the two most critical moments in the golf swing, as far as elbow tendonitis is concerned, are, first, the transition from the backswing to the downswing, where the stretching is greatest, and, second, the moment of impact, where the jolt is greatest (13).

Advice from the Experts

In his chapter on elbow injuries in *Feeling up to Par—Medicine from Tee to Green*, Dr. William Stannish looks at each phase of the golf swing, identifies where the elbow is particularly at risk during each phase, and provides some pointers for avoiding injury (13). Advice from several other sources is also included:

Pregame Preparation and Equipment Selection

- Use the more flexible graphite shafts, or switch to a low-compression ball (90 instead of 100), to lessen the impact on the elbows.
- Practice on real turf instead of rubber mats, which seems to deliver less of a jolt. (This one comes from me!)

The Address

- Ease up on grip tension, and loosen the elbows, to lessen strain on the forearm flexors and extensors (32).

The Backswing

- Bring the club back *slowly*, to minimize the stretch and strain placed on the forearms and wrists and to reduce the momentum of the club. With a "one-piece" take-away technique, there is minimal strain on the elbow because the wrists move only a little.

- Maintain correct positioning at the *top* of the backswing, and make a *smooth transition* to the downswing. This is critically important. At the top of the backswing, the golfer exerts the wrists and forearms to reverse the direction of the club and initiate the downswing. Adopting a slow and smooth backswing allows the wrists to cock naturally and reduces strain on the wrists and elbows.

- Initiate the forward arm motion with the *shoulders/trunk*, to avoid the "casting maneuver," a premature release of the hands at the top of the backswing. Casting the club into the swing (much the same way a fishing rod is casted, using the wrists) is a common flaw in swing technique. The hands/wrists should not release until impact with the ball. In addition to placing excessive strain on the elbows, forearms, and wrists, casting is bad for your golf game too, frequently resulting in a *slice* of the ball (13)(26).

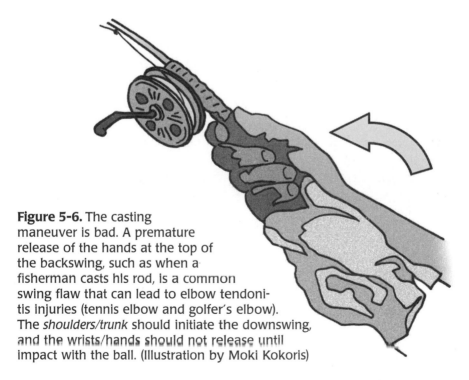

Figure 5-6. The casting maneuver is bad. A premature release of the hands at the top of the backswing, such as when a fisherman casts his rod, is a common swing flaw that can lead to elbow tendonitis injuries (tennis elbow and golfer's elbow). The *shoulders/trunk* should initiate the downswing, and the wrists/hands should not release until impact with the ball. (Illustration by Moki Kokoris)

The Downswing

- During the downswing, resist the temptation to *decelerate* the swing as a means of maintaining club head control just before impact. Holding the wrists back places undue strain on the forearms and puts the elbow at risk. Allowing the club's momentum to swing through the ball and uncock the wrists naturally will help reduce elbow and forearm injuries (13).

The Impact

- The moment of club impact with the ball is the phase most associated with golf injuries of all types, including elbow injuries. At impact, the right forearm flexors and the left forearm extensors are both firing away like mad to overcome the counterforce of ball impact. This is the point at which the golfer is at high risk for developing *golfer's elbow on the right side* and *tennis elbow on the left side*. Therefore, players with chronic elbow (or wrist) pain should—

- Adopt a more elliptical swing (so the ball is *swept* off the grass without taking a divot (31). Taking a divot, or hitting a fixed object such as a rock or tree root, greatly increases the counterforce of impact, and the risk of elbow tendon strain (13)(7).

- Use the more flexible graphite shafts, or switch to a low-compression ball, to lessen the strain of impact on the elbows.

- Ask their partner if he or she will allow you to tee-up the ball on fairway shots as well. This will lessen the chance of taking a divot. (If your partner is kind enough to let you get away with that, I suggest you buy them the beer in the clubhouse! Friends like that are hard to find.)

The Follow-Through

- The follow-through phase of the swing is relatively elbow-friendly. The stresses on the wrists and elbows seen during the downswing and impact phases have lessened significantly by the time the follow-through is reached.

Parting Shots:
The Elbow

Elbow tendonitis (tennis elbow and golfer's elbow) is by far the most common elbow injury among golfers. The golf swing places repetitive stresses on the forearms, the elbows, and the wrists, which—coupled with poor swing mechanics—can lead to chronic and disabling injury.

Successful elbow-injury prevention focuses on:

- Basic conditioning. Once muscles fatigue, the stage is set for excessive tendon strain and injury. Regular strengthening exercises can minimize fatigue of the forearm flexors and extensors during play and practice.

- Warm-up and pregame stretching. Warmed-up tendons and muscles perform better and are less prone to injury. A thorough warm-up should be part of every player's routine, regardless of skill level.

- Swing mechanics. Consult your local golf pro for advice about improving your swing mechanics, especially if you're returning from an elbow injury.

- Equipment. Consider equipment changes, such as more flexible shafts or a low-compression ball, especially if you are returning to play after an elbow injury.

- The backswing. Slow down the backswing. Make a smooth transition from backswing to downswing.

- The downswing. Save the "casting" for the trout stream. Do not initiate the downswing with the wrists. Avoid club deceleration on the downswing.

- Impact. Do not take big divots, and avoid hitting fixed objects with the club head—it's murder on the elbows. If you find your ball is lying so close to a tree root or rock that you are likely to hit it with your club, do yourself a favor and *move the ball a little.* Tell your partner that Dr. Divot, M.D. told you to.

Wrist and Hand Injuries

Chipper is a fifty-three-year-old teacher at the local driving range. For the last six months he's been having problems with his left hand. He complains of a constant "bruised" feeling in the palm near the base of his index finger. It bothers him when grips his club. For the last three months, he's noticed that the finger is "stuck" when he gets up in the morning. He has tried over-the-counter medication, but the problem hasn't gone away.

Golf causes a significant number of injuries to the wrist and hand, including fractures, tendonitis, and nerve injuries. And it's interesting that the frequency of wrist and hand injuries differs among various groups of golfers. Female professional golfers are particularly prone to wrist and hand injuries (which amount to about one-third of the injuries to women). Male professionals suffer wrist and hand injuries at about half the rate of their female counterparts. Amateur golfers (both male and female) also encounter a significant number of hand and wrist problems.

Wrist and Hand Anatomy 101

The bony anatomy of the wrist begins with the two forearm bones: the *radius* and the *ulna*. The eight *carpal* (wrist) bones come next, arranged in two rows. The "wrist joint" is not a single joint at all, but rather is a complex assembly of many small joints. Each of the irregularly shaped carpal bones interlocks with its neighbor like pieces of a jigsaw puzzle. A complex array of ligaments tethers the bones together, providing stability.

This complicated and delicate arrangement gives the wrist joint significant mobility. The wrist can flex/extend, rotate palm-down and palm-up (pronate/supinate), and tilt from side to side (radial and ulnar deviation). All these motions come into play during the golf swing.

The hand is comprised of the tubular *metacarpal* and finger bones (phalanges). Simple hinge joints in the fingers allow only flexion and extension. The thumb, however, has a more sophisticated joint mechanism and therefore has more mobility than the fingers. Because of this mobility, the joint at the base of the thumb (the basal joint) is a frequent site of arthritis.

Straightening (extension) of the wrist and fingers is performed by extensor muscles and tendons located on the top of

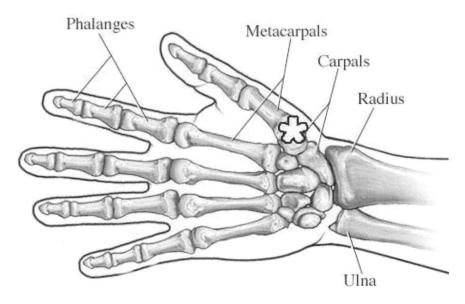

Figure 6-1. Basic hand and wrist anatomy. The wrist is composed of the two forearm bones (the *radius* and the *ulna*), and the eight *carpal* bones arranged in two rows. Next come the *metacarpal* bones and the *phalanges* of the hand and fingers. The *basal joint* (*) at the base of the thumb is capable of more motion than the simple hinge joints of the fingers and is a common site of arthritis. (Copyright 2003 Nucleus Medical Art, all rights reserved. www.nucleusinc.com)

the forearm/wrist/hand. The flexors bend the wrist and fingers down and are located on the palm side.

Several golf-related hand and wrist problems occur with sufficient frequency to merit individual consideration: DeQuervain's tendonitis, ECU tendonitis and ECU tendon subluxation, the wrist impaction syndromes, wrist flexor tendonitis, trigger finger, fracture of the hamate bone, and carpal tunnel syndrome.

DeQuervain's Tendonitis

One quite common form of wrist tendonitis, named after Swiss surgeon Fritz deQuervain (1868–1940), affects golfers and nongolfers alike. Women, particularly mothers of newborns, are especially prone to develop the condition.

DeQuervain's tendonitis involves injury to a group of tendons located along the end of the forearm near the base of the thumb. These tendons pass through a tight tunnel of bone and ligament as they cross the wrist on their way to the thumb, and it is within that tunnel that the tendons are susceptible to injury. Repetitive side-to-side motions of the wrist are especially irritating. Why do new mothers get deQuervain's tendonitis? It

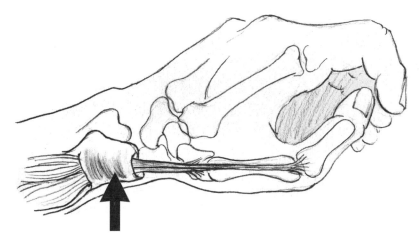

Figure 6-2. DeQuervain's tendonitis of the wrist. A group of tendons located along the end of the forearm near the base of the thumb are susceptible to injury as they pass through a tight tunnel of bone and ligament (arrow). (Illustration by Suzanne AuBuchon)

seems that the position in which mothers hold their wrists while feeding and lifting Junior causes tendon inflammation.

In golfers, deQuervain's tendonitis tends to involve the *left wrist*. Excessive cocking of the left wrist on the backswing, and rapid deviation of the wrist in the opposite direction at impact, are believed to be the causes (14). Further stress on the tendons occurs in players with poor mechanics who perform the casting maneuver at the top of the backswing. (Recall that the casting maneuver was also previously implicated as a cause of elbow tendonitis.) Pain is felt along the thumb-side of the wrist at the top of the backswing and at the initiation of the downswing.

Evaluating a patient for deQuervain's tendonitis:

- Pain (usually gradual in onset), tenderness, and swelling are localized to the wrist near the base of the thumb. Occasionally, if the tendons are particularly swollen, a clicking sensation is felt as the wrist and thumb are moved about.

- Numbness and tingling are absent.

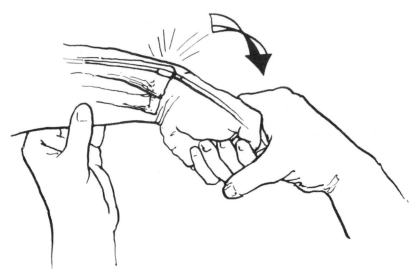

Figure 6-3. The Finkelstein test for DeQuervain's tendonitis. In golfers with DeQuervain's tendonitis, deviation of the wrist away from the thumb will be painful as the inflamed tendons at the wrist are stretched. (Illustration from Stover CN, McCarroll JR, Mallon WJ (eds): Feeling Up to Par: Medicine from Tee to Green, p 155 with permission.)

- X-rays are normal but can rule out the presence of arthritis in the nearby wrist or base of the thumb.
- The classic test for deQuervain's tendonitis is the Finkelstein test. Here, the patient is asked to loosely grasp the fingers around the thumb while the examiner deviates the wrist away from the thumb. When I suspect a patient has deQuervain's tendonitis, I save this test for last because it usually makes them jump off the table.

Most doctors have pretty big egos and would love to be immortalized like Doctors Finklestein and deQuervain by having a disease or a test named after them. Maybe a hundred years from now a golfer will say, "Good gravy, Loretta, that's your fifth triple-bogey today. Maybe you should see your doctor—you've got *Foster's syndrome.*"

I find deQuervain's tendonitis easier to treat than tennis elbow or golfer's elbow. Treatment options include:

- Rest, ice, and anti-inflammatory medication, if symptoms have been present for only a short time (a few days to a couple of weeks), may help clear things up quickly.
- Splinting is also helpful, to rest the inflamed tendons. The standard wrist splint used to treat carpal tunnel syndrome won't do the trick. With deQuervain's tendonitis, the thumb must be splinted as well, requiring a thumb spica splint. While a thumb spica splint is fairly user-friendly for most daily activities, it is too bulky and restricting to be worn while playing golf.
- Hand therapy aimed at lowering local tendon inflammation can help, then stretching and strengthening exercises are emphasized.
- DeQuervain's responds particularly well to cortisone injection, and I have had many patients whose symptoms are resolved with a single injection.
- Most cases respond well to nonsurgical measures. For patients with persistent pain despite appropriate nonsurgical treatment, surgery is considered. The surgery involves a

simple procedure through a small incision in which the ligament roof overlying the inflamed tendons is opened to give the tendons more "breathing room." Experts recommend that golf be resumed *gradually* a month or so after surgery. Initially, short-game practice only is recommended, with no backswing above the level of the waist. After another few weeks, full participation can resume (14)(26).

ECU Tendonitis

The ECU (extensor carpi ulnaris) tendon is also susceptible to repetitive injury and tendonitis from golf. This tendon is located along the pinky side of the wrist near that knobby bump at the end of the ulna bone.

Though it is much less common, ECU tendonitis is similar to deQuervain's tendonitis in many ways. Pain and tenderness are localized over the inflamed tendon. Appropriate nonsurgical treatment includes rest, NSAID medication, wrist splinting, and perhaps cortisone injection. In rare cases, surgery is necessary to obtain pain relief (26). And the high-handicap player who utilizes the casting maneuver is again at risk.

ECU Tendon Subluxation

The ECU tendon is also susceptible to another golf-related injury that can result from repetitive overuse or as the result of even a single bad shot. Here, the delicate sheath of tissue surrounding the ECU tendon is torn or stretched, destabilizing the tendon and allowing it to slide back and forth (sublux) with a painful clicking sensation.

This injury can occur when a golfer takes a fat shot, or accidentally strikes a tree or a root or a rock, for example. The sudden deceleration of the club forcefully twists the wrist, injuring the tendon sheath. ECU tendon subluxation can also result from gradual stretching of the tendon sheath over time due to overuse.

Nonsurgical treatment includes immobilization in a brace or cast that extends above the elbow for about one month, followed by another month of wrist-splinting. If the tendon sheath fails to heal properly, surgical repair is recommended (14)(26).

Wrist Impaction Syndromes

The repetitive and extreme ranges of motion that a golf swing demands of the wrists can lead to what are called "impaction syndromes" of the wrist, where the bones literally bang into one another when there is excess wrist motion. For example, repeated and excessive right-wrist extension during the golf swing can lead to injury due to impaction between the carpal bones and the radius.

On examination, tenderness is present at the site of impingement—for example, in the case of dorsal impaction syndrome, on the top of the wrist. X-rays may reveal a small bone spur at the site of injury.

Treatment generally includes rest, splinting, and possibly cortisone injection. Surgery is rarely necessary. Swing modifications, such as slowing down the backswing to minimize wrist extension at the top of the backswing, may help to prevent or relieve the problem (14).

Wrist Flexor Tendonitis

The main wrist-flexor tendons, the FCR (flexor carpi radialis) and the FCU (flexor carpi ulnaris), are also prone to overuse injury and tendonitis and can give the golfer problems. These tendons are located along the palm side of the wrist.

With wrist-flexor tendonitis, pain and tenderness are localized to the involved tendon. Standard treatment recommendations include rest, avoidance of golf, NSAID medication, splinting, and exercises. Nonsurgical treatment is usually successful (26).

I had one interesting case of a golf-related FCR tendon injury in a patient who had contracted polio as a child and had to play golf one-handed. He actually ruptured his FCR tendon while playing golf.

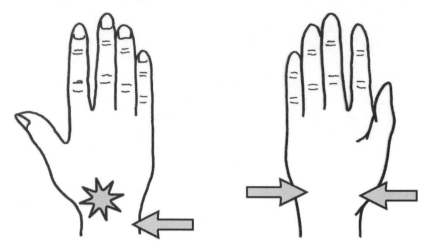

Figure 6-4. Other types of wrist tendonitis and wrist impaction syndrome. The ECU tendon is located along the pinky side of the wrist (arrow, left image) near the knobby bump at the end of the ulna bone. The ECU tendon can become inflamed or sublux from repetitive injury or from a single fat shot. Dorsal wrist impaction causes pain along the top of the wrist (star, left image). The FCR and FCU tendons are located along the flexor (palm) side of the wrist (arrows, right image) and are occasional sources of tendonitis for the golfer. (Illustration by Moki Kokoris)

Trigger Finger
(Flexor Tendonitis of the Finger)

A common form of tendonitis that affects both golfers and nongolfers involves the flexor tendons of the fingers. This is what my patient Chipper has. As the flexor tendons travel from the palm to their respective fingers, they pass through a tunnel of fibrous tissue called the "flexor tendon sheath."

This sheath both lubricates and nourishes the tendon and holds the tendons close to the finger bones to prevent the tendons from bow-stringing away from the bone. The sheath is like the rings on a fishing rod that keep the fishing line (that is, the tendon) close to the rod as the line glides back and forth. Without the rings, each time a fish was caught the line would bow-string away from the rod, rendering the rod ineffective.

A "trigger finger" occurs when a flexor tendon becomes inflamed, resulting in a thickening in the tendon. The inflammation also causes the first portion of the tendon sheath to thicken.

The net result is that a thickened tendon is trying to fit through a narrowed tunnel. As a result of this mismatch, a painful catching (triggering) of the tendon occurs as it pops through the bottleneck in the sheath as the finger is flexed and extended. To return to the fishing-rod analogy, imagine the fishing line has a knot in it and that each time the knot passes the first ring on the rod it snags momentarily.

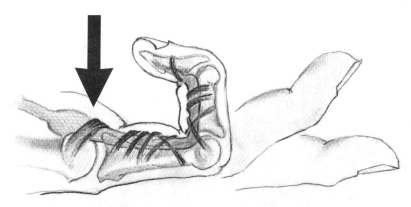

Figure 6-5. Trigger finger. The finger flexor tendon glides back and forth in the tendon sheath. A *trigger finger* occurs when a thickened and inflamed tendon gets caught as it passes into the sheath (arrow). In the fishing-rod analogy, the fishing line has a knot (thickened tendon) that gets snagged on the ring (sheath) as it glides back and forth. (Illustration by Suzanne AuBuchon)

Symptoms of a trigger finger usually evolve gradually—first some mild soreness in the finger and palm, then the onset of painful triggering of the finger. Most patients do not recall a specific injury. It has been speculated that golf contributes to the formation of trigger fingers through a combination of repetitive overuse and trauma to the flexor tendons from the golf swing, which result in tendon inflammation and thickening (26).

In the golfer, the left hand once again takes the brunt of the abuse. First, less-skilled players tend to exert too much pressure with the left hand because they feel the need for the left arm and hand to *drive* the club through the swing. Furthermore, many amateurs play with the *strong grip position*, where the left hand is rotated clockwise on the club handle. This points the "V cre-

ated by the left thumb and index finger toward the right
shoulder. In this position, the
club handle rests right under
the knuckles in the palm, which
also happens to be the location
of the most vulnerable (bottleneck) segment of the flexor
tendon and sheath (26).

Evaluating a patient for trigger finger is usually easy:

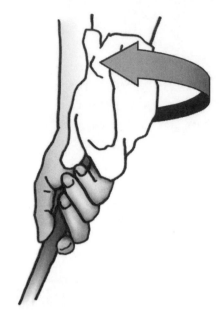

- A tender thickening
  along the tendon in the
  palm is common. As the
  patient makes a fist, the
  finger locks, and then
  pops when the finger is
  extended again. The
  locking and triggering
  tend to be most notice-
  able in the morning.

- The middle or ring fin-
  ger and/or the thumb
  are most frequently in-
  volved.

Figure 6-6. The strong grip position. A contributing cause to finger ten-donitis and trigger fingers is use of the *strong grip* position. In this posi-tion, the left hand is rotated clockwise on the club handle. When this occurs, the handle rests directly under the knuckles in the palm where the bottleneck portion of the flexor tendon and sheath is located. (Illustration by Moki Kokoris)

- Certain medical conditions (gout, rheumatoid arthritis, diabetes) are associated with a higher rate of trigger fin-gers.

- Numbness and tingling are absent.

- X-rays are normal.

Treatment is directed at eliminating the root cause of a trig-ger finger: a mismatch between the thickened tendon and the narrowed tunnel (sheath). In other words, to cure the triggering we can try to shrink the tendon's swelling, or make the tunnel bigger (41).

The anti-inflammatory effect of cortisone injected into the tendon sheath can shrink the tendon swelling enough to eliminate the triggering. Sometimes, though, relief obtained from a single injection is only partial or temporary. In that case, a second cortisone injection can be considered. Repeated injections, however, raise the risk of tendon-weakening and rupture.

If nonsurgical treatment fails, a safe and simple surgical cure is available for trigger finger. Under local anesthesia and through a tiny incision, the first part of the narrow tendon sheath is opened up, thereby eliminating the triggering. Patients can then usually resume golf in four to six weeks.

Fracture of the Hamate Bone

Unless you are in the habit of punching your golf partner in anger, chances are you will never sustain a wrist or hand fracture while on the golf course. The golf swing is much more likely to result in soft-tissue injuries, such as tendonitis brought on by overuse and repetitive stress.

One exception, however, is a golf-related fracture of the hamate bone in the wrist (14). The hamate bone is positioned in the second row of carpal bones on the pinky side of the wrist. The hamate has a small prominence, called the hook, which juts into the palm. A deep blow to the palm puts the hook of the hamate at risk for fracture. For the right-handed golfer, the butt end of the club rests over the hamate in the *left* palm. Any forceful deceleration of the

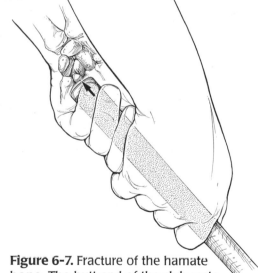

Figure 6-7. Fracture of the hamate bone. The butt end of the club rests over the hamate bone in the left palm. Hitting a fat shot or object, such as a tree root or rock, can result in fracture of the vulnerable *hook* of the hamate bone (arrow). (Copyright 1992 John M. Daugherty)

club, as when hitting a fat shot or striking a rock or tree root, for example, can result in a fracture of the hamate hook. A hamate hook stress fracture can also result from repeated stress rather than a single injury (14)(15)(16).

It is interesting that hamate hook fractures also occur in baseball and tennis by a similar mechanism. Like the golf club, both the tennis racquet and the baseball bat are held with their butt ends over the hamate. Former home-run king Roger Maris is reported to have sustained a hamate hook fracture that plagued him throughout his sub-par 1962 season. Not until after the season ended was the correct diagnosis made.

A golf-related hamate fracture is painful—so painful that the injury-producing shot will likely be the last shot of the day, and possibly the last shot of the golf season! Despite the initial pain, however, a fractured hamate is frequently be dismissed by the injured player as a bruise. It is not uncommon for patients to wait weeks or even months to seek medical attention. Only when that painful "bruise" continues to cause pain with each attempted golf shot does the injured player go see a doctor.

Evaluating a patient for a hamate hook fracture:

- A fractured hamate hook can easily be missed on first examination, because the injury is relatively rare and because this fracture is almost impossible to detect on routine X-rays of the wrist.
- Specialized imaging tests, such as a CT scan or an MRI, may be the only way to see this tiny but pesky fracture.
- Nearby tendons can fray on the rough bone edge, resulting in flexor tendon rupture. In addition, nearby nerves can be injured, resulting in numbness/tingling and weakness in the hand (14)(15)(16)(26).
- Most hand and wrist fractures seen in orthopedic practice can be successfully treated with immobilization (a cast or splint), but a fractured hamate hook is an exception. The track record for healing a hamate hook fracture with casting is not good. That is why some authorities advise that surgical removal (excision) of the fractured

tip be the first treatment of choice. After surgery, patients can typically return to golf in eight to ten weeks.

As with most sports injuries, prevention is the key. I think of my vulnerable and innocent hamate bone every time I address a ball that has come to lie too close to a fixed object, such as a rock, a sprinkler head, or a tree root. I then do something I'm not ashamed of: *I move the ball to the nearest spot that will afford me a safe swing, and I tell my playing partners I am doing that to avoid breaking my wrist.* I also insist that my partners do the same when their ball lies near a dangerous object. (When playing with my brother Gregg, that can include parked cars, fire hydrants, and vending machines.)

I know, I can hear some of you sticklers for the letter of the law crying "Foul!" To me, though, golf is for fun—and fun only. The day I take the game so seriously that I stand by and let my partner take a dangerous shot rather than give him a little slack is the day I get a new hobby. Those of you who want to be macho about it have been forewarned.

Carpal Tunnel Syndrome

One of the most common clinical problems I see in orthopedic practice is carpal tunnel syndrome (CTS). I'm sure you or someone you know has suffered from CTS. In the United States alone, well over 100,000 people a year undergo carpal tunnel surgery. It is such a common disorder that it's amazing doctors have so little understanding about what actually causes carpal tunnel syndrome.

We do know that carpal tunnel syndrome is associated with certain medical conditions, such as diabetes, thyroid disease, and gout. Furthermore, it is widely believed that repetitive use of the hands and wrists causes carpal tunnel syndrome. (It is being seen with increased frequency among people with certain occupations, such as butchers, grocery clerks, and factory workers.) However, no scientific study has ever proven a direct link between any specific job activity and carpal tunnel syndrome.

The truth is that the causes of CTS are what we doctors call multifactorial. That is, multiple factors, including occupational and recreational overuse, underlying medical conditions, genetics, and who knows what else, all contribute to this very common syndrome (42).

Although playing golf has not been identified as a direct cause of carpal tunnel syndrome, the repetitive use of wrists and hands seen in golf could certainly contribute. But to say that playing a few rounds of golf a month is a major factor in the development of your carpal tunnel syndrome is probably stretching the point. The same may not be true for the serious amateur or pro, for whom the countless hours of practice and play could take its toll. In the foreword he wrote for the book *Feeling up to Par,* golf pro Ken Venturi notes that he developed such severe carpal tunnel syndrome in both hands that his career was ended (14).

Carpal tunnel syndrome occurs as a result of an injury to the median nerve. As this nerve travels from the forearm to the wrist, it passes through a structure called the carpal tunnel. Just like New York's Lincoln Tunnel and Holland Tunnel, the carpal tunnel has a ceiling and a floor. (For those of you unfamiliar with New York, these two tunnels connect the Big Bad City with the beautiful Garden State, New Jersey, where I was raised.) The wrist bones form the floor of the tunnel, and the ceiling is made of a thick ligament. Packed into the tunnel, along with the median nerve, are most of the flexor tendons en route to the fingers.

When inflammation and swelling of the tendons in the tunnel cause crowding and increased pressure on the median nerve, carpal tunnel syndrome is the result. The pressure on the nerve causes it to malfunction, causing the symptoms of CTS.

Patients with carpal tunnel syndrome describe several classic symptoms. Numbness and tingling involving the thumb and the index and middle fingers, and sometimes the whole hand, are the hallmark of CTS. Annoying numbness can occur both during the day (while doing things such as driving, holding a telephone, or using hand tools) and at night (patients are frequently awakened from sleep by numbness in the hands).

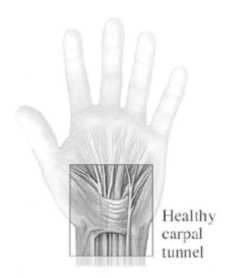
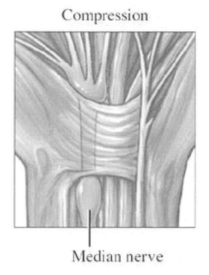

Compression

Healthy carpal tunnel

Median nerve

Figure 6-8. Carpal tunnel syndrome. As the median nerve travels from the forearm to the wrist it passes, along with most of the flexor tendons, through the *carpal tunnel* (left image). Inflammation of the nerve and tendons leads to crowding in the tunnel and pressure on the nerve from the overlying ligament roof of the tunnel (right image). (Copyright 2003 Nucleus Medical Art, all rights reserved. www.nucleusinc.com)

Clumsiness and weakness when trying to grip things are also common complaints. There may be pain as well.

Evaluating a patient for carpal tunnel syndrome:

- Tapping on the nerve with a fingertip (the Tinel sign) will cause an electrical sensation into the fingers of the patient. Holding the wrist in a flexed position for 30 seconds or so will induce tingling in the fingers (the Phalen test). Both tests serve to tweak an already irritated median nerve and provoke abnormal sensations in the CTS patient.

- Sensitivity to light touch testing in the thumb, index, and middle fingers (the territory of the median nerve) may be diminished.

- Weakness and wasting of the muscles at the base of the thumb may be seen in advanced cases of CTS.

- Other signs of tissue inflammation (such as trigger fingers) may be present.
- Nerve tests (called electrodiagnostic studies) can be used to confirm the diagnosis of CTS and to rule out other common causes of numbness in the hand (such as a pinched nerve in the neck).

A course of rest, wrist-splinting (especially at night), and NSAID medication are frequently the initial treatments for carpal tunnel syndrome. Identifying work-related or recreational activities that may be aggravating the situation is also helpful. Looking for ways to get the job done using less force, less repetition, and/or less wrist motion may help. These measures are most successful for early and mild cases.

Studies show that only about one-third of patients will respond to these simple measures. For the rest, surgery may be the only answer—or, as one of my former co-residents used to say, the only cure left is hot lights and cold steel!(42).

The concept behind CTS surgery is simple—the tunnel is "unroofed" by cutting the ligament overlying the nerve. This gives the nerve extra breathing space that is usually sufficient to allow the injured nerve to recover and for symptoms to resolve. In the early 1900s, surgeons mistakenly believed that carpal tunnel syndrome was caused by pressure on the nerves at the base of the *neck* and that the treatment was rib resection. Ouch! For those of you who constantly long for the "good old days," I recommend that you stick to reminiscing about five-cent Hershey bars and leave out the early days of medicine. As Carly Simon says, *these* are the good old days!

Surgery can be performed either through an open incision or through tiny incisions with the aid of a camera (endoscopic technique). Either way, the success rate of CTS surgery is very high. Postoperatively, patients can return to golf once the incision is healed and wrist strength and range of motion have returned to normal.

Wrist and Hand Injuries and the Golf Swing

The majority of golf-induced wrist and hand injuries are *overuse* injuries, such as tendonitis. Excessive play and practice, poor swing technique, and mis-hits involving the ground or objects (roots, etc.) have all been associated with wrist and hand injuries in the amateur golfer (5).

Swinging a golf club properly demands more motion from our wrists than most daily activities. During an average normal swing, the right wrist flexes and extends through an arc of about 100 degrees of motion and undergoes about 45 degrees of side-to-side motion. The left wrist undergoes less flexion/extension (about 70 degrees) than the right wrist, but slightly more side-to-side motion (10).

Research indicates that continuing to play once a wrist or hand is injured may lead to further injury. One study compared healthy golfers with those suffering from an injury to the wrist, hand, or forearm (10). It is not surprising that when forearm and wrist strength were compared, the injured golfers were found to be significantly weaker. Furthermore, the injured golfers had less wrist range of motion when tested while they were performing nongolf tasks. This all makes sense. You would expect an injured wrist to be weaker and have less range of motion than a healthy wrist.

However, detailed swing analysis has revealed that injured golfers exhibited *more wrist motion* when swinging a golf club than the healthy subjects did. But why, when swinging a golf club, does an injured wrist move more than an uninjured one? One theory is that the weakness injured golfers experience may render them unable to resist the forces imposed on the wrist by the golf swing, resulting in excessive wrist motion. It is as if, in the case of a golfer with a wrist injury, *the club swings the golfer,* and this may lead to even further injury (10).

In addition to the high motion demands made on the hands and wrists during the golf swing, a significant amount of force is transmitted to the hands from the club at the moment of impact. The left hand, in particular, takes a real beating.

Advice from the Experts

To help reduce the risk of injury, the golfer can take numerous precautions and make modifications in the swing:

Equipment Selection

- Use club grips that are larger and softer, to help minimize trauma to the hands. Furthermore, because playing with worn club grips can require increased grip pressure, casual players should consider getting their clubs rewrapped yearly. Serious players, who play more frequently, should rewrap their clubs every 40 or 50 rounds (26).

- Use a glove on *each* hand to provide helpful extra cushioning.

- Check for proper club length. When club lengths are correctly fitted, the butt end of the club handle should extend beyond the fleshy pad on the pinky side of the left hand. Clubs that are too short place the butt of the club directly against the hook of the hamate bone, putting that bone at risk for fracture (26).

Figure 6-9. Proper club fitting. When club length is properly fitted, the butt end of the handle extends *beyond* the fleshy pad in the pinky side of the left hand. Clubs that are too short place the butt of the club in the palm directly against the vulnerable hook of the hamate bone. (Illustration from Stover CN, McCarroll JR, Mallon WJ (eds): Feeling Up to Par: Medicine from Tee to Green, p158 with permission.)

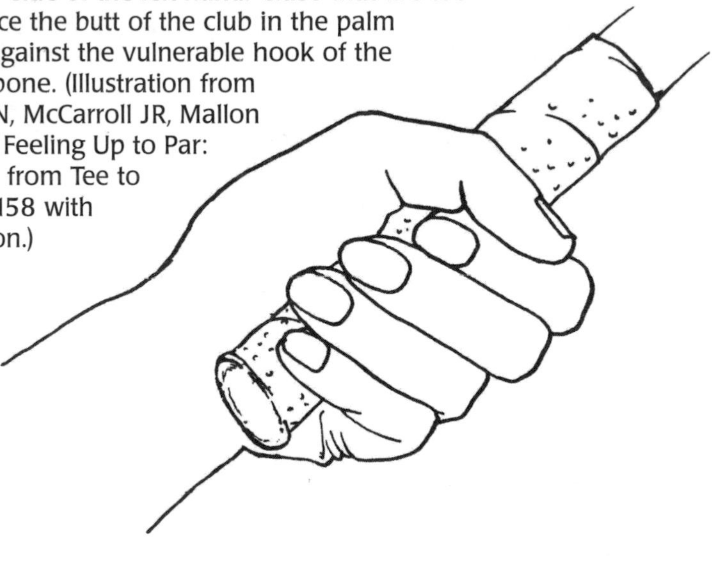

The Address

- Reduce the grip pressure during the address phase, to decrease stress and strain on the hands, wrists, and forearms.

- Avoid the strong grip position in order to lessen the pressure on the flexor tendons in the palm. Rotating the left hand more counterclockwise will position the club handle more diagonally in the palm and keep it from pressing directly against the flexor tendons and sheath.

The Backswing

- The *left wrist*, at the top of the backswing, is maximally cocked in the direction of the thumb. This wrist position has been implicated as a cause of wrist tendonitis (deQuervain's tendonitis) and can aggravate pain in the left thumb for patients who have arthritis in the thumb basal joint. The *right wrist*, at the top of the backswing, is hyperextended, which makes it susceptible to impaction syndrome.

- Avoid excess wrist motion (left wrist cocking and right wrist hyperextension) at the top of the backswing by *slowing down the backswing.* This lowers the momentum of the club and makes the club less likely to force the golfer's wrists into extreme positions.

- Initiate the downswing with the shoulders/trunk, and avoid premature release of the hands and wrists at the top of the backswing. Remember our old nemesis, the casting maneuver when making the transition from backswing to downswing. The hands should not release until the moment of impact, to avoid placing excessive strain on the wrists, as well as the forearms and elbows.

- Adopt a more elliptical swing line, so that the ball is *swept* off the turf, to lower the likelihood of taking a divot at impact. A swing with a steep swing plane is more likely to result in taking a jolting divot later in the swing.

Impact

- Never swing at the ball if it is sitting close to a rock, a tree root, or any other obstruction. Most hand and wrist injuries occur in the impact phase. At the moment of contact, the left hand receives a jolt from the club. Hitting a fat shot or striking a fixed object with the club can result in several serious acute hand injuries, including fracture of the hamate bone and tearing of the ECU tendon sheath (ECU subluxation).

Follow-Through

- At follow-through, both wrists are again cocked in the direction of the thumb. The left forearm and wrist *supinate* (assume the palm-up position), and the right forearm and wrist *pronate* (rotate into the palm-down position), to create the "roll-over" motion of the hands. The follow-through is believed to be the swing phase least associated with wrist and hand injuries (4)(7)(14)(26).

Parting Shots: The Wrist and Hand

The wrist and hand account for a significant number of golf-related injuries. Excessive play and practice, poor swing mechanics, and mis-hits involving the ground or fixed objects are common causes of injury.

Successful wrist and hand injury prevention should include:

Basic conditioning. Strong and well-conditioned muscles are able to continue performing longer and better than poorly conditioned muscles. Once fatigue sets in, the stage is set for accelerated tendon strain and injury of the wrists and hands.

Warm-up and pregame stretching, to enhance performance and decrease the risk of injury.

Smart equipment selection, such as clubs of appropriate length, padded grips, and gloves.

Avoidance of swing technique pitfalls, such as the strong grip position, excessively rapid backswing, and the casting maneuver.

Keep in mind that continuing to play with a wrist or hand injury may lead to excessive wrist motion during the swing, and risk further injury.

Hitting a tree or rock with the club can cause a season-ending hand injury, such as fracture of the hamate bone. Don't try to be John Wayne and hit a ball from a dangerous spot. Let's be practical: Most of us stink at this game anyway. Does it *really* make a difference if we move the ball a little? I'm not advocating deception or cheating—merely the tacit agreement among friends to look out for one another's safety.

Back Pain and Spine Injuries

Richard is a seventy-year-old patient of mine. He is such nice man, and his old-school upbringing is refreshing. He always comes in meticulously dressed—shined shoes, pressed slacks, sweater and tie—and a golf hat. Even after he changes into his paper gown he still manages to look dignified. (Maybe it's because he keeps the golf hat on!). I always spend an extra few minutes with Richard, talking about golf. His eyes light up. He even offered to take me and my son golfing with him. He wasn't just making small talk either. He was being sincere.

On one occasion Richard came to see me for his back. He shuffled down the hall, slightly hunched over on his way to the exam room. When I greeted him and asked him how he was, he still managed a smile and said, "I'm doing fine, Doctor Foster. No complaints."

When we got to our customary golf discussion, Richard told me his back was so sore he couldn't take his full swing without pain. "It hurts in my lower back when I twist, and sometimes into my backside." (He would *never* use the word "butt.") He also mentioned that he'd lost mobility in his back over the years and that he couldn't swing the club the way he used to.

Richard is in good company. At one time or another in their careers, Jack Nicklaus, Tom Kite, Fuzzy Zoeller, and Fred Couples all had significant back injuries that threatened their ability to tour (1)(12). In fact, back pain in golf is so common that the topic takes up a sizable portion of this book.

Surveys reveal that the lower back is the most common area of injury among male PGA golfers, and the second most common injury site among female golf professionals. One survey of Japanese professional golfers revealed that more than 50 percent reported a history of low back pain that forced them to skip tour events or kept them from competing effectively (55). Amateur golfers also list the lower back as their most frequent problem area (1)(2).

Spine Anatomy 101

The human spine is a wonderful but complicated structure that is a frequent source of pain for the golfer. The bony spinal column runs from the base of the skull to the tip of the tail bone. The spinal column is made up of stacked vertebral bones: 7 neck (cervical) vertebral bones, 12 chest (thoracic) vertebral bones, 5 lower-back (lumbar) vertebral bones, the sacrum, a large triangular bone, forming the back portion of the pelvis, and the tailbone (coccyx), at the lower end of the spine. Most of our later discussion of back pain will focus on the lumbar spine because that is where most injuries occur.

The vertebral bones of the neck, chest, and lower back all share a similar basic design. The cylinder-shaped *body*, the largest part of a vertebral bone, is designed for weight-bearing. A protective bony tunnel, for the spinal cord and nerves to pass through, is behind the stacked vertebral bones.

Little Mickey Mouse ear-shaped structures sticking up and down from each vertebral bone lock each vertebral bone to its neighbors from above and below. Tiny joints (facet joints), formed where the vertebral bones interlock with their neighbors, stabilize the spine. (These joints are frequent sites of painful arthritis, particularly in the older golfer.) Another bony tunnel is on each side of every vertebral bone through which a left and right spinal nerve passes—more on this later (2)(25)(43).

Ligaments, which provide stability and help control motion between the segments of the spine, bind the vertebral bones to one another. Some ligaments run the entire length of the spine, others are designed to stabilize and support the tiny facet joints.

The musculature of the spine is truly complicated. For some reason, this area in gross anatomy gave me fits in medical school—too many complex layers of muscle, and each with its own obscure Latin name. It made my head hurt. Take my word for it—there are *a lot* of spinal muscles.

These spinal muscles, together with the abdominal muscles, make it possible for the spine to flex, such as when bending over to pick up your golf ball; to extend, as when arching your back to yawn while your partner fidgets for five minutes preparing to putt; to bend to the side (lateral bending); and to rotate, as when turning around to yell at your kids in the back seat.

A main function of the spine is to protect the nerve tissue of the spinal cord. The spinal cord itself is a rope-like bundle of countless millions of tiny nerve fibers that runs from the base of the brain to the lumbar spine. The cord is

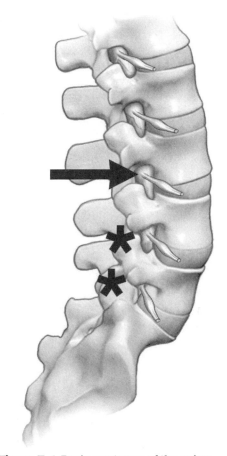

Figure 7-1. Basic anatomy of the spine. This side view of the lumbar spine shows the stacked *vertebral bones*. The cylinder-shaped body of the vertebral bone is designed for weight-bearing, while the *facet joints* (*) interlock the vertebral bones. The *discs* are durable structures that act as cushions between the vertebral bones. The *spinal cord* travels within a protective bony tunnel behind the vertebral bones. *Spinal nerves* exit the spine through small bony tunnels on either side of the vertebral bone at each level of the spine (arrow). (Copyright 2003 Nucleus Medical Art, all rights reserved. www.nucleusinc.com)

protected from harm by a bony tunnel behind the vertebral bones.

As the spinal cord travels down from the brain, spinal nerves at each vertebral level exit the spine through a small bony tunnel on either side of the vertebral bone. Overall, there are thirty-one pairs of spinal nerves (eight cervical, twelve thoracic, five lumbar, five sacral, and one coccygeal). As the spinal cord travels farther down the spine, the cord becomes narrower, because more and more nerve tissue has been rerouted as spinal nerves. Once spinal nerves exit the spine, they group together to form the main nerves, which then travel to the arms and legs (for example, the ulnar and sciatic nerves, respectively).

The discs are major components of the spine. Each vertebral bone in the spine is joined to its neighbor by a disc. These disks are tough, durable structures formed by an outer layer of criss-crossing fibers (we can liken these to the nylon and steel plies in an automobile tire) and an inner core of proteins, carbohydrates, and water. The inner core, which acts like a very dense sponge, provides a hydraulic cushion between the vertebral bones.

As we age, the water content of the discs decreases, and the discs lose their pliability and resilience (1)(43). Just as the shocks on a car wear out with time, the discs (the shock absorbers of the spine) also wear out with age.

The Back and the Golf Swing

During a golf swing, the discs and other components of the spine are subjected to tremendous stresses, including:

- Compression
- Rotation (twisting, torsion)
- Shear
- Bending

To illustrate how these different stresses act on the spine, let's use what I call the Oreo cookie model—developed by yours truly after decades of dedicated research eating countless cookies on my couch. Now, imagine an Oreo cookie on steroids, where

the cookie wafers are much thicker than normal—these represent the two neighboring vertebral bones. The cream filling
between the two wafers, also much thicker than normal, represents the disc.

As any Oreo lover knows, you go for the cream filling first,
using one of several methods. Let's translate those methods to
disc-talk:

- If you squeeze the wafers together in an attempt to squash
  the cream out the sides, you are *compressing* the disc.
- If you try to unscrew the cookie by twisting the wafers in
  opposite directions, you are applying *rotation (torsion)
  stress* to the disc.
- If you try to slide the wafers in opposite directions to
  uncover the cream, *shear stress* would come into play.
- If you pry one wafer off another by tilting the top wafer,
  you are applying *bending stress* to the disc.

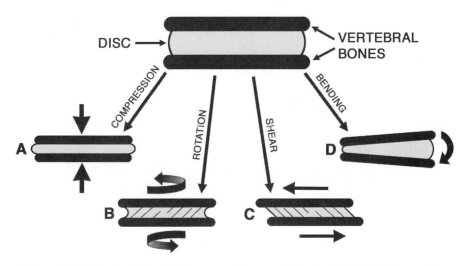

Figure 7-2. Doctor Divot's Oreo cookie model helps illustrate the various
stresses a golf swing puts on the spinal discs. *Compression* acts to squash
the disc. *Rotation* stress (torque) twists the disc. *Shear* is a side-to-side stress.
Bending stress occurs when one half of the disc is stretched while the other
half is compressed. (Illustration by Moki Kokoris)

Now, let's see if we can put everything together and sum up the important points about the anatomy of the spine:

- The human spine is a highly specialized and complex structure that has two main functions: It protects the delicate nerve tissue of the spinal cord, and it transfers loads and stresses from the head and trunk to the pelvis.

- The spine undergoes various immense stresses, even during routine activities. Several sources contribute to that stress: body weight, muscle activity, a rubber band-like elastic loading from spinal ligaments, and externally applied loads (such as the stress imposed by heaving a golf bag and clubs into a particularly uncooperative water hazard).

- The spine maintains its stability using a complex array of supporting muscles, ligaments, the facet joints—and the ever-important discs (1)(12)(43).

Back Pain on the Back Nine: Back Injury and Treatment

Okay, you may ask, if the human spine is such an exquisitely designed masterpiece of engineering, then why does my back *hurt* so much?

Good question. I own a 1955 Buick. (My old car is the one vestige of my carefree youth that I didn't toss onto the scrap heap the day I got married.) My Buick is also well engineered, but it still spends a fair amount of time in the shop. The bones, discs, joints, muscles, and ligaments of the spine are subjected to a lifetime of stresses and abuse. Unfortunately, unlike our cars, there is no Mr. Goodwrench who can replace the worn parts—and nothing approaching a lifetime warrantee where the spine is concerned.

Back pain affects all people, not just golfers. It strikes about eight out of ten adults at some time in their lives and is the leading cause of lost work time. In fact, its cost to society (due to lost wages, decreased work productivity, and treatment) reaches billions of dollars each year.

You'd think that any medical condition that affects hundreds of millions of people worldwide each year would be well understood. The truth is, however, our understanding of back pain and its causes is shockingly rudimentary. But research continues (56).

Back pain is a condition that doctors refer to as being *multifactorial*. That is, multiple factors (some obvious, some not) appear to contribute in a complicated way to the development of back pain. For instance, episodes of acute low back pain in adults have been linked to several "risk factors," (56):

- A previous history of low back pain
- Advancing age
- A history of smoking
- Heavy physical work
- Job dissatisfaction

But you may be wondering how something like hating your job or smoking cigarettes can lead to back pain. Well, puzzling and unexpected data like this make it difficult for researchers, too, when trying to understand back pain.

The next logical question, for golfers, is whether *golf* causes low back pain. As you can see, what seems like a simple and straightforward question is actually extremely difficult to answer, because of the many risk factors we *all* have for developing back pain.

One interesting study on the subject of golf and back pain came from the Netherlands. (I didn't know they played golf there, did you? I'll bet their water hazards are doozies!)

Novice golfers, ages twenty-two through sixty were surveyed both at the beginning and at the end of their first year playing golf. The authors' goal was to identify a causal link between back pain and playing golf. Some of the relevant findings for these NetherDuffers included (3):

- More than 60 percent of the golfers had a prior history of back pain (mostly low back pain) before taking up golf. This fact reinforces just how common back pain is in the general population, golf or no golf.

- Eight percent of players who never had back problems before reported having their first bout of back pain during their first year playing golf.
- Forty-five percent of players who had a prior history of back problems before taking up golf noted a recurrence of back pain during their first year of golfing.
- Golfers who participated in multiple sports, in addition to golf, were twice as likely to report back problems.

The authors concluded that their limited study was unable to confirm that playing golf leads directly to back pain. Statistics and science are nice, but I *know* that playing golf is a killer for my lower back. I'll bet golf is tough on your back too. If golf does not cause low back pain, then it sure as shootin' *aggravates* back pain caused by other factors in life.

Types of Back Pain

Back pain can be broadly categorized based on the structures in the spine that are injured. Because the lower back is most frequently the site of pain and injury among golfers, we'll focus on the lumbar spine, the lower back.

Lower Back Pain

Some of the more common types of low back pain include:

- Mechanical back pain, which is generally attributed to injury to the muscles and ligaments of the lower back
- Disc-related low back pain
- Back pain due to arthritis of the lumbar spine
- Stress fractures of the lumbar spine

Mechanical Back Pain

Mechanical back pain is caused by injury to muscles and ligaments of the spine (and there are lots of them). This type of injury is probably the most common cause of back pain, and eventually almost everyone experiences mechanical back pain to some degree.

Evaluating a patient with mechanical back pain:

- Pain is localized to the lower back, without radiation of pain, numbness, or weakness to the legs.
- The pain usually increases with physical activity and decreases with rest.
- On physical exam, patients with mechanical back pain exhibit decreased range of motion of the spine due to pain and muscle spasm.
- Reflexes, sensation, and muscle strength in the legs are normal (indicating an absence of nerve involvement).
- X-rays of the spine are normal. (However, muscle spasm can sometimes cause *increased straightening* of the lumbar spine on X-ray).
- Fancy imaging studies (such as MRI or CT scans) are not really helpful in working up a case of mechanical back pain. First, these tests typically are not sensitive enough to "see" which muscle or ligament is actually injured. Second, the results of these expensive tests are unlikely to alter the doctor's treatment strategy in the earliest stages.

Treatment for mechanical back pain includes:

- Rest. I tell my patients to use common sense and to employ the concept of *relative rest*. This means that their activity level should fall somewhere between what they routinely do and complete inactivity. Most doctors no longer encourage their patients to go home and spend three weeks in bed, because too much inactivity seems to lead to increased stiffness. On the other hand, rotating the tires on your car, lugging that old sofa to the basement, or *playing golf* are all likely to lead to more trouble.
- Medications, such as NSAIDs, muscle relaxants, or a brief course of narcotic pain medication (for severe cases) can help take the edge off the discomfort.
- Physical therapy can help patients with lingering mechanical low back pain. In general, patients find the modalities (heat, ultrasound, etc.) soothing. The therapist then em-

ploys stretching and strengthening exercises to maximize spinal and abdominal muscle strength and flexibility, and to improve body mechanics.

Fortunately, most episodes of mechanical back pain seem to resolve as mysteriously as they come on. Most patients are better within a few weeks—with or without a doctor's treatment. I'm convinced that the most helpful thing I do for patients who are in the midst of an acute episode of back pain is to reassure them that the odds are great that they will recover soon without any heroic intervention from doctors.

Disc-Related Back Pain

As we get older, the discs in our spine lose their resiliency and ability to absorb and distribute spinal stresses. This is largely due to an *age-dependent loss of water content* within the discs. Furthermore, a rupture of the outer fibers of the disc can cause

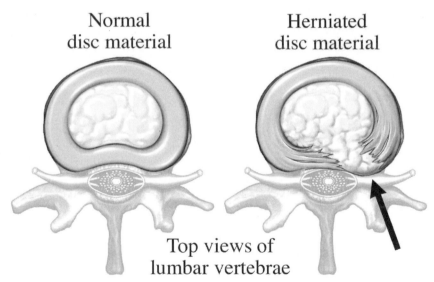

Figure 7-3. Spinal disc herniation. The image on the left shows a normal disc as seen from above. With a *herniated* (or *slipped*) disc, the outer fibers of the disc rupture, allowing the central disc material to escape (right image). Pressure from the herniated disc material can then irritate and injure the nearby spinal nerve (arrow), leading to symptoms of pain, numbness, tingling, and weakness down the leg. (Copyright 2003 Nucleus Medical Art, all rights reserved. www.nucleusinc.com)

the central disc material (commonly referred to as a "slipped" or "herniated" disc) to escape. Here's where we run into trouble. The disc material can herniate backward into the bony tunnel where the spinal cord and spinal nerves live. Pressure from the herniated disc material can then irritate and injure the nearby spinal nerve(s), leading to all sorts of problems.

The *pattern* of abnormal signs the physician finds in his examination serves as a clue to which spinal nerve (and disc) is the culprit. That is, when a spinal nerve from a particular level in the spine goes haywire, it will produce a specific set of symptoms.

Based on these symptom, or "clues," the doctor can often deduce (just like Sherlock Holmes) which disc and nerve are injured, even before fancy tests, such as an MRI, are performed.

Evaluating a patient for a "slipped" disc:

- Pain can occur not only in the back but also *down the leg.* The pain can be accompanied by other symptoms of spinal nerve irritation and injury, such as numbness, tingling, and muscle weakness in the leg. The poor leg is an innocent bystander here.

    In essence, the injury to the spinal nerve in the lumbar spine causes a short-circuit of the nervous system and fools the brain into perceiving pain in a remote part of the body—in this case, the leg. There really is no injury to the leg, but the injury to the nerve *going to the leg* causes the brain to misperceive the pain, numbness, and tingling as coming from the leg.

    This is a phenomenon doctors call "referred pain." Because of the way our nervous systems are wired, we sometimes feel symptoms in areas far away from the actual site of injury. The same thing occurs when a heart attack victim complains of pain in the left arm (or, like when my daughter and wife go to the mall, I feel pain in my wallet).

- Coughing, sneezing, or bearing down to go to the bathroom frequently aggravate the back and/or leg symptoms from a slipped disc, because all these activities increase the pressure the disc puts on the nerve.

- Symptoms may come on either suddenly or gradually. Sometimes the patient will know exactly where and when the injury occurred because of the sudden onset of symptoms ("There I was, Doc, bending down to pick up my ball on the thirteenth green and—*Wham!*"). Other times, patients experience a more gradual onset of symptoms. One patient may come to the office wondering what that annoying tingling in her big toe is all about, while another patient may literally crawl into the emergency room pleading to be put out of his misery.

- Bowel or bladder incontinence may signal the presence of a more serious nerve injury problem that requires more aggressive treatment.

- X-rays, however, while helpful as part of the overall physician work up, will *not* reveal a disc herniation. The discs (as well as the other soft tissues, such as muscles and ligaments) are not visible on routine X-rays, so don't let anyone tell you they see a herniated or slipped disc on your X-ray. They can't. The only thing that can be seen on an X-ray is the space where the disc lives, not the disc itself.

- The MRI (magnetic resonance imaging) scan has become the standard method for confirming the presence of a herniated or slipped disc. Using magnetic energy, the MRI can create detailed images of the bones and of the soft tissues (such as the discs, nerves, spinal cord, and muscles). The scan can help confirm the diagnosis the physician has already made based on an assessment of the clues at hand. The MRI pictures are also helpful in planning future treatment, such as surgery.

- Other tests that can help evaluate a disc herniation include the CT (computerized tomography) scan and the myelogram (a test in which dye is injected around the spinal cord and a MRI or CT scan is then performed).

- Special nerve tests (typically performed by a neurologist) can also be useful in determining which nerve is injured and to what degree.

Treatments for a diagnosis of disc herniation include:

- Rest, medication, and reassurance. Early treatment strategy for a slipped disk is similar to that of mechanical back pain: —"relative rest," medication (NSAIDs, narcotics), and reassurance are the logical start. It's not well understood why, but the symptoms of a slipped disc can subside on their own within a few weeks or months.

- Physical therapy modalities. Exercises, and heat, ultrasound, and other therapy options can sometimes help.

- Oral steroids. A short course of oral steroid medication to try to break the cycle of nerve irritation sometimes helps.

- Cortisone injection. A series of cortisone injections directed into the spine (epidural steroid injections) can help with more persistent or debilitating disc symptoms, but such injections do not always provide complete or permanent relief. However, they are safe, and a relatively painless way to help patients without resorting to surgery.

- Surgery. I always reassure my patients that the great majority of patients with a slipped disc do not go on to require surgery. In fact, only about 20 percent of herniated disk patients ultimately need surgery.

- The indications for surgery to remove a slipped disc are quite strict. Only patients who have not reached a satisfactory level of pain relief and function despite a reasonable trial of nonsurgical treatment should be considered. Furthermore, surgery is considered only if a specific clear-cut anatomic abnormality that explains the patient's symptoms is identified (1)(12).

Back Pain from Arthritis of the Lumbar Spine

Back pain due to arthritis is another common cause of back problems for the golfer, particularly the older player. Remember the facet joints, those tiny joints formed between neighboring vertebral bones? They work like those little ridges on poker chips, allowing the stacked vertebral bones to interlock.

The facet joints are primarily responsible for resisting shear stress (side-to-side sliding) in the spine. The loads borne by the facet joints in the lumbar spine are especially increased with spine hyperextension (arching of the back).

Advancing age and the repeated stressing of the facet joints can result in degeneration and arthritis of the facet joints. The cartilage lining and supporting ligaments and capsule of the joints can degenerate, resulting in stiff and painful facet joints at multiple levels in the spine.

Evaluating a patient with arthritis of the lumbar spine:

- Patients typically complain of a vague, dull, or aching discomfort deep in the lower back, and sometimes into the buttocks and upper thigh.
- Patients often note that their pain increases with walking and is relieved somewhat with rest.
- Physical examination reveals a decrease in lumbar spine range of motion, and discomfort when the physician presses on (palpates) the involved facet joint(s).
- If there is extensive facet joint disease, the resulting formation of bone spurs can press on nearby spinal nerves and cause pain, numbness/tingling, and weakness down the leg (producing a clinical picture similar to that of a slipped disc).
- X-rays, CT scans (which give excellent details of the bones), and MRI scans can all be used to evaluate lumbar spine arthritis.

Treatment for lumbar spine arthritis includes:

- Early on, rest and medication.

- A supportive brace can also help, but spine braces can be a double-edged sword. On the one hand, the brace can provide pain relief by limiting motion in the arthritic joints. However, the spine tends to compensate for this by increasing motion in the areas just beyond the brace. This increased motion in neighboring spinal segments could theoretically result in injury there (1)(12)(23).

- A therapist-supervised trunk-strengthening rehab program should be considered when the acute discomfort has eased.

- More aggressive treatments, such as injections or surgery, are reserved for the most nagging and debilitating cases.

Back Pain from Stress Fractures in the Lower Back

The last major type of back pain stems from an injury to a segment of the vertebral bone called the *pars,* which is designed to support the facet joints. So-called *stress fractures* can occur in the pars when, over time, repeated stress is placed on the bone. Research has shown that the amount of shear stress placed on the lower back during the golf swing is about the same as the amount of stress needed to cause fractures of the pars in laboratory cadaver studies (1).

Evaluating a patient with a stress fracture of the lumbar spine:

- Pain is usually localized to the lower back, without leg symptoms.

- The pain is typically increased with lumber spine hyper-extension.

- Routine X-rays may not reveal the stress fracture. Other diagnostic tests, such as a CT scan, an MRI scan, or a bone scan may be required to detect a subtle stress fracture of the pars.

- In extreme cases of pars injury, one vertebra will slip forward on its neighbor due to a loss of structural support for the shear-resisting facet joints (a condition called spondylolisthesis).

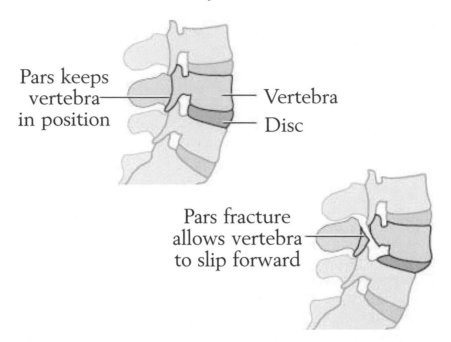

Pars keeps vertebra in position

Vertebra

Disc

Pars fracture allows vertebra to slip forward

Figure 7-4. Pars fracture and back pain. Repeated stress to the *pars* portion of the lumbar spine (such as from the golf swing) can lead to painful *stress fractures*. If the injury to the pars is severe, the shear-resisting facet joints lose their structural support, allowing one vertebra to slip forward on its neighbor—a condition called *spondylolisthesis*. (Copyright 2003 Nucleus Medical Art, all rights reserved. www.nucleusinc.com)

Treatment for stress fractures of the spine includes:
- Rest and medication (are you starting to notice a pattern?).
- Therapy to tone and condition the abdominal and trunk muscles. Theoretically, this can take some of the stress from the pars and the other bony portions of the spine.
- Bracing.
- Surgery, but reserved for severely debilitating cases.

Overall, the incidence of back pain due to a true stress fracture of the pars is rather rare, compared with the more prevalent types of back pain (mechanical, disc-related, and arthritis-related low back pain). For duffers like me, it's the lack of "pars" on my scorecard, rather than the pars in my spine, that makes the game of golf so painful at times.

The *real* world of back pain and its treatment is considerably more complicated than it sounds, though. First, there are numerous causes of low back pain that I did not cover (spinal stenosis, inflammatory diseases, compression fractures, and on and on). Second, sometimes back pain can be a symptom of a problem occurring *outside* the spine (for example, a dangerous aneurysm of the aorta in the abdomen can sometimes be felt initially only as back pain). Finally, it is important to keep in mind that the spine can have more than one thing wrong at the same time—for example, a bad disc *and* arthritis of the facet joints.

For successful, and safe, treatment of back pain, proper diagnosis is important. This requires that your physician take a complete history of the problem, conduct a detailed physical exam, and obtain the appropriate diagnostic tests, before treatment begins.

Low Back Pain and the Golf Swing

Now that we have a basic understanding of the spine and back pain, we can focus our attention on the mechanics of the golf swing and how the golf swing relates to back pain.

We all know that the game of golf had its origins in Scotland. In fact, my brother and I are convinced that we are descendents of at least two Scottish noblemen—Sir Duffalot and the Earl of Doublepar. In the early days of the game, the style of play was decidedly different than it is now. Clubs had supple "whippy" shafts made of hickory. Historic players, such as Bobby Jones, utilized the "classic swing," which differs from today's "modern swing" technique in several important ways:

- The classic golf swing begins with a flatter swing plane than the modern swing.
- The classic backswing employs both a generous hip turn and a shoulder turn, such that both the hips and the shoulders rotate nearly equally.
- During the classic backswing, the player rises up on the left toe.

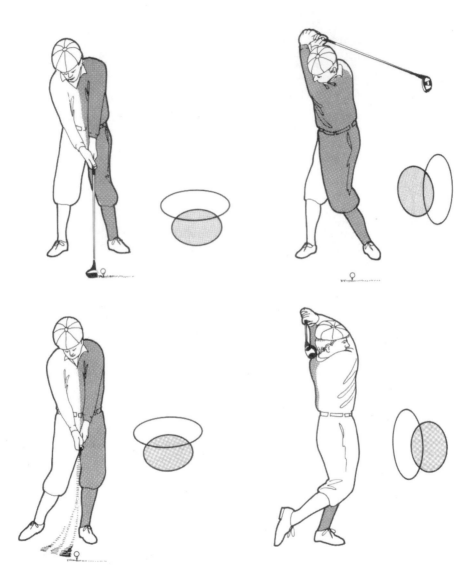

Figure 7-5A. The classic golf swing. The *classic* golf swing is characterized by a flatter swing plane, a generous turn of both the hips *and* the shoulders, and a follow-through that ends with a straight-up-and-down "I" position. The shaded oval depicts the position of the hips, and the unshaded oval depicts the position of the shoulders. Note how the hips and shoulders rotate together. (Illustration from Stover CN, McCarroll JR, Mallon WJ (eds): Feeling Up to Par: Medicine from Tee to Green, p99 with permission.)

Figure 7-5B. The modern golf swing. The *modern* golf swing is character-ized by a large shoulder turn and a restricted hip turn. The follow-through finishes with a "reverse-C" posture and a hyperextended spine. The ovals again depict the position of the hips (shaded oval) and the shoulders (un-shaded oval). Note how the shoulders rotate much more than the hips. (Illustration from Stover CN, McCarroll JR, Mallon WJ (eds): Feeling Up to Par: Medicine from Tee to Green, p100 with permission.)

- The classic swing follow-through finishes in an upright and relaxed "I" position.

By contrast:

- The modern golf swing utilizes a more vertical (up and down) swing plane.
- The modern swing combines a large shoulder turn with a restricted hip turn. By limiting the hip turn and maximizing shoulder rotation, the spine and shoulder muscles store energy like a giant coiled spring. That energy is then released—uncoiled—in a sudden burst during the downswing.
- During the modern backswing, the left foot is kept flat on the ground.
- The modern swing finishes with what has been described as a "reverse-C" posture characterized by a hyperextended spine.

The modern golf swing was developed to take advantage of club design improvements (steel and now graphite shafts, metal club heads) and to maximize power, distance, and accuracy. With your modern golf swing, you can launch your thirty-dollar-per-dozen liquid plutonium-centered balls farther than Bobby Jones ever dreamed possible—but at a price. The stressful mechanics of the modern golf swing have been implicated as a major contributor to golf-related injury, particularly to the lower back. The excessive twisting of the lower spine, followed by the sudden de-rotation and hyperextension of the spine, are believed by experts to be too stressful for the average golfer, and even for the pro (1)(2)(7).

We become so accustomed to watching top professional athletes play on television that we forget how incredibly gifted they truly are. They make it look so easy that we are lulled into the belief that anyone could do what they do. We can't. As a kid growing up in New Jersey (Exit 135), I dreamed of pitching like Tom Seaver. Then, as part of my midlife crisis, I joined a men's thirty-and-over hardball league, and I learned a lot from that. I learned that I stink at baseball even more than I stink at golf. Since discovering how difficult it is to hit a curveball, even one thrown at me by someone just as old and paunchy as I am, I've developed a greater respect for pro ball players. The same is true for pro golfers. I watch Tiger Woods play with his grace and power and say to myself, "I can do that." But I can't. Nobody has called me "Tiger" since my wedding night—and nobody ever will, on the golf course.

What, then, are the differences between professionals like Mr. Woods, and amateurs (that's putting it very politely) like you and me? For one thing, every time Tiger hits the ball it threatens to go in the cup. Every time I hit the ball, it threatens the life of the girl driving the hot dog cart on the neighboring fairway!

All kidding aside, there are some fascinating research results that illustrate distinct differences between professional golfers and amateur golfers. Much of this research focused on issues involving the lower back, and it sheds some light on why the lower back is such a problem area for both the golfing pro and the weekend warrior.

Doctors Timothy Hosea, Charles Gatt, and Eric Gertner have undertaken a detailed biomechanical analysis of the golf swing in both professional and amateur golfers. They measured muscle activity during the golf swing, using a device called a myoelectrogram. Surface electrodes (like those used for an EKG), were used to determine which muscles were firing (contracting) at various phases of the golf swing. Furthermore, the intensity of those muscle contractions was calculated and compared with what those muscles would be capable of producing during a maximal (peak) contraction. In short, the studies found out *which* muscles were firing during the golf swing and *how hard* those muscles were firing.

Next, Dr. Hosea and his colleagues used muscle activity measurements, video swing analysis, and computed modeling to calculate the stress forces generated at the lumbar spine during the golf swing for both the professional and amateur golfer. The results confirm that swinging a golf club is very stressful to the lower back and its muscles. The data also illustrate that there is a distinct difference between the pro and the amateur (1)(2).

First, the shear, bending, compression, and rotation stresses acting at the lumbar spine during the golf swing were calculated in units called Newtons (N). (Recall how we used the Oreo cookie model to demonstrate the different ways these stresses affect the spine.) The results are surprising:

- The peak shear and bending stresses on the lumbar spine during the golf swing were found to be 80 percent greater in the amateurs than in the pros (560 N vs. 329 N for the shear stress). For comparison, the peak shear stress on the lower back was calculated for other strenuous sports, including male rowing (848 N) and squat lifting (690 N).

- Compression stresses on the lower back during the golf swing were calculated to exceed *eight times* the stress of body weight for pro and amateur alike. In laboratory cadaver studies, this is just about the amount of compression stress it takes to cause a disc to *rupture!* For comparison, compression stresses on the lower back were calculated to be three times body weight during running, and seven times body weight during rowing.

- Rotational stresses were calculated in units called Newton-meters (Nm). For the professional, a peak of 56.8 Nm was calculated, compared with 85.2 Nm for the amateur. The *transition from the backswing to the downswing* was noted to be the portion of the swing that produced the greatest rotational stress on the lower back. The medical literature has linked rotational stress to the development of back pain (1)(2).

Dr Hosea's research team uncovered how the typical swing pattern of the amateur golfer leads to increased bending stresses on the lower back. They found that amateurs tended to not transfer enough of their weight to the right side during the takeaway, but rather kept too much weight concentrated on the left foot. The team also found that, at the top of the backswing, amateurs tended to throw their arms and shoulder outside the plane of the swing, and then had to compensate by bending the trunk to the left to bring the upper limbs and club head back to meet the ball. The amateurs were actually leaning away from the ball at impact. (2)

Professional golfers, on the other hand, experienced lower bending stresses on the lower back because they exhibited a more complete weight shift to the right foot during the take-away, and because they kept their arms and shoulder within the plane of the swing at the top of the backswing. This more efficient swing made it possible for the professionals to achieve the proper position of leaning into the ball at impact (2).

These research results are not here just to bombard you with lots of fancy numbers. What's important is getting a sense of what these studies show—that the golf swing imposes stresses on the spine comparable to those seen in other demanding sports activities, such as running, rowing and weightlifting. I'd wager that if similar calculations were made for other strenuous sports activities, the golf swing would be near the top of the list. The other important point is that amateurs generate more stress on their lower backs during a golf swing than do professionals!

So, even though golf is considered by some to be a gentleman's game, and not a real sport, the truth is that golf is really tough on the body. Failure to appreciate this fact sets us up for serious injury if we forget to respect the game for what it is—a strenuous sport that demands basic conditioning, pregame warm-up, and attention to proper swing technique.

The myoelectric data Dr. Hosea and his associates gathered yielded equally thought-provoking results:

- While the professional golfers exhibited a spinal/trunk muscle activity of 80 percent of their maximum during their swings, the amateurs reached nearly 90 percent of their maximum. Recall that muscle activity is a major contributor to stresses affecting the spine. These data, therefore, illustrate that the golf swing demands a *near all-out muscular effort*, particularly from the amateur.

- In amateurs, the muscular firing pattern was imprecise, but in the tested professionals the firing pattern reflected a discrete on-and-off profile.

At first glance, such studies can be confusing and seem contrary to common sense. How can a professional golfer—someone who hits the ball harder, farther, and straighter than I do—actually use less of his total muscle capacity, and generate less stress on the lower back, than I do? The answer is that the pro is a conditioned athlete with an efficient, "grooved" swing. Going back to baseball, when Tom Seaver threw a fastball, he did so with machine-like efficiency. (I used to love the way his knee would get dirty.) If *I* were to stand on a mound and attempt to throw a baseball 90 miles an hour, my arm would fall off.

Why should golf be any different? We as hackers should realize that the top physical conditioning of professionals like Tiger, combined with superior mechanics (and, let's throw in a little natural talent), allow him to do things we can't do. The greatest thing about golf as a hobby is that *you don't have to be that good at it to still have fun,* and I'm living proof of that. Try being "not too good" at hang-gliding and see where that gets you.

You might be wondering why professional golfers, in spite of their superior conditioning and swing technique, still manage to hurt their backs so frequently. The answer is probably in the high number of times that they swing the club each week. One review of elite Japanese golfers revealed a high incidence of low back pain on the right side, and X-ray evidence of early arthritis in the right lumbar spine. These findings were attributed to the highly repetitive and asymmetric stresses of the golf swing, particularly during the impact and follow-through phases of the swing (55). Even the most sophisticated and finely tuned machine will eventually begin to show signs of wear.

Advice from the Experts

What, then, are some of the key concepts and recommendations we can gather from the available orthopedic research? In his chapter titled "Back Pain: Diagnosis and Treatment" in the book *Feeling up to Par,* Dr. Ned Brooks Armstrong makes the following useful observations and recommendations (12).

Pregame Preparation and Equipment Selection

- Develop and maintain strength and flexibility of the spine/trunk, buttocks, and thighs. This, in combination with age- and ability-appropriate aerobic conditioning (for example, walking, biking, swimming), can make the golfer less prone to injury. The abdominal muscles (such as the oblique muscles), in particular, work with the spine muscles to support and stabilize the spine during the golf swing. Weakness and fatigue of the abdominal and spinal muscles leads to excessive stress and wear on the bones, ligaments, and discs (71).
- Use proper back mechanics to avoid stress on your lower back, not only when swinging the club but also while doing other activities. For example, when getting your golf bag out of the trunk, avoid bending at the waist and leaning into the trunk to hoist your bag out. Instead, maneuver your bag to the edge of the trunk and lift it using your *legs* as well as your back.
- Avoid bending forward at the waist when teeing the ball or retrieving the ball from the cup. Squatting through the knees places much less stress on the lower back, whereas bending at the waist and keeping the knees straight is a real killer for the lumbar discs.
- On the greens, use a putter with a longer shaft, or adopt an upright posture while putting. This avoids the kind of bending that puts stress on the lower back.

The Address

- Proper "athletic" positioning from the start of the golf swing is important to the execution of both a successful (good) shot and a safe shot.
- Weight should be comfortably distributed onto the balls of both feet. The width of the stance varies depending on the shot being made (53). For long shots, with a driver,

the feet will be farthest apart—a little more than shoulder-width apart. For shorter shots, with an iron, the feet will be slightly closer together. In any case, placing the feet too far apart will limit the hip turn later in the swing, which we know places greater rotational stress on the lower back.

The Backswing

- Today's modern golf swing, though designed to maximize power, results in increased and potentially dangerous stresses on the spine.

- Remember that rotational stress on the lower back, in particular, has been linked to low back pain. The greater the difference between the shoulder turn and the hip turn, the greater the rotational stress on the lower back.

- Adopt a more "classic" swing technique—where the hips and shoulders turn more equally—in order to significantly decrease the rotational stress on the lower spine. Today's modern golf swing, though designed to maximize power, results in increased and potentially dangerous stresses on the spine.

- Slow down the backswing to reduce the body's backward momentum and possibly reduce the rotational stress on the lower back as the coiled spinal "spring" begins to uncoil. Remember that it is the *transition* from the backswing to the downswing that places the most rotational stress on the lower back.

- Dr. Hosea's research has showed us that proper weight shift to the right foot on the take-away and keeping the arms and shoulder within the plane of the swing at the top of the backswing will help the golfer decrease bending stresses on the lower back (2).

The Follow-Through

- Use the "classic" follow-through, which employs a more relaxed upright "I" position that places less stress on the lower back. The modern golf swing emphasizes hyperextension of the lower back at the end of the follow-through (the "reverse-C" position), but excessive extension (hyperextension) of the lower back causes increased stress on the bones, discs, ligaments, and muscles of the lower back.

Parting Shots: The Lower Back

The spine, the lower back in particular, is one of the most frequent locations of golf-related injury.

All golfers—professional and amateur, female and male—report a high incidence of back problems.

The discs and other structures of the lower back are subjected to significant stresses including compression, rotation, shear, and bending during the golf swing.

Professional golfers tend to develop low back pain due to repetitive overuse from excessive play and practice.

Amateur golfers may be at risk for back pain due to improper swing technique and poor conditioning. During the golf swing, amateurs stress their muscles more, and generate higher stresses in the lower back than do professionals.

The "modern" golf swing employed by professionals emphasizes extreme spine rotation on the backswing, and spine hyperextension on the follow-through, which is believed to contribute to high spine stress and injury.

Adopting a "classic" swing technique, which limits spine rotation and hyperextension, may reduce the risk of back pain for the amateur player.

Lessons from a golf pro can help you to adopt the modifications noted above into your own golf swing.

Maintaining overall body fitness may decrease the risk of back injury. Maximizing flexibility and strength of the spine/trunk muscles, and the muscles of the buttocks and legs, can decrease the amount of stress placed on the spine.

Paying attention to proper back mechanics (such as squatting through the knees instead of bending through the lower back) will spare the lower back from unnecessary stress.

Dr. Armstrong makes the important point that recurrent lower back problems, in both athletes and nonathletes, are most commonly due to *not allowing sufficient time for the injury to heal*, and to a *lack of appropriate rehabilitation* before resuming pre-injury levels of activity (12). Ongoing back problems should be evaluated and treated by a doctor.

Finally, if you do adopt the "classic" golf swing, keep in mind that the knickers and goofy hat are strictly optional.

Shoulder Injuries

Carl is a thirty-two-year-old salesman who entertains many of his clients by taking them golfing. Golf is not only fun for Carl—it's a business necessity. For six months, Carl has had pain in his left shoulder and upper arm. "Yeah, you've got it," he said as I slowly raised his arm over his head, reproducing his pain.

At first, it was only an annoying ache at the end of a round. Now, the shoulder bothers Carl when he reaches for his seatbelt in the car. He is finding it increasingly difficult to sleep through the night. Carl is concerned because he has a big convention coming up in Las Vegas and he wants to take his biggest clients out for a day of golf. "Give me a pill, give me a shot—I don't care—just get me better so I can play golf next month."

Figuring out what Carl's problem is will take some medical detective work, and the solution may not be as simple as he hopes. What we commonly refer to as the "shoulder joint" is actually a series of several joints working in unison. This complicated mechanism is designed to allow us to position our hands in space. One important job of the shoulder is to bring the arm into the overhead position, as when serving a tennis ball. Athletes who participate in these "overhead" sports tend to miss a significant amount of playing time due to shoulder problems. In fact, an alarmingly high percentage of overhead athletes, including high-level swimmers (66 percent), professional pitchers (57 percent), college volleyball players (44 percent), and college javelin throwers (29 percent), have documented shoulder problems.

Fortunately, the rate of shoulder injuries among both pro and amateur golfers is relatively low, because of the relatively shoulder-friendly mechanics of the golf swing. And golf is not considered an overhead sport. A five-year survey of players on the Senior PGA Tour revealed that the shoulder accounted for about 7.7 percent of the total injuries reported (36). Other large-scale studies of both pros and amateurs also indicate that the shoulder comprises about 10 percent, or less, of all reported golf injuries (4)(5)(6)(33).

Shoulder Anatomy 101

The shoulder contains three bones: The humerus is the bone in the upper arm. The shoulder blade (scapula) is a flat, triangular bone that lies against the ribs in the upper part of the shoulder. The collarbone (clavicle) is a tube-shaped bone that acts as a strut between the breastbone (sternum) and the shoulder blade.

The upper part of the humerus has a ball-shaped *head* that glides around in a socket on the shoulder blade. This is the "main" shoulder joint.

A small joint (called the acromio-clavicular, or "A-C" joint) is formed where the collarbone and shoulder blade meet. Other joints are formed where the shoulder blade meets the chest and where the collarbone meets the breastbone.

Seventeen (yes, seventeen) different muscles are involved in shoulder motion. For the golfer, some of the most important are:

- The rotator cuff, which is made up of four different muscles that originate on the front and back surface of the shoulder blade. The four muscles then form a common *cuff* of tendon tissue (the rotator cuff tendon) that then anchors into the head of the humerus. Depending on which of the muscles is firing, the humerus is made to rotate one way or another in its socket. Hence the catchy name: a cuff of tendon that rotates the humerus—*rotator cuff.* The rotator cuff muscles are critical for performing overhead activities and for swinging a golf club.

- The deltoid muscles, strong muscles that are key to performing many overhead activities.
- The pectoral muscles ("pecs"), strong muscles that form the main part of the chest and help bring the arm back *down* from the overhead position.
- The latissimus muscles ("lats"), which also help bring the arm back down from the overhead position.

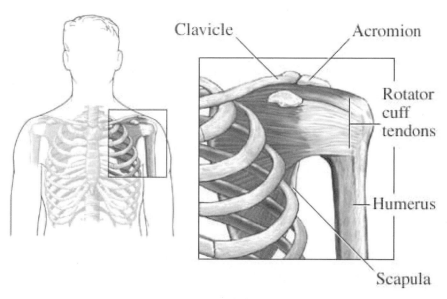

Figure 8-1. Basic shoulder anatomy. The main shoulder joint is a ball-and-socket joint formed by the round upper humerus and a socket on the shoulder blade. The *rotator cuff* is a key structure for the golf swing. Four different muscles originating from the shoulder blade form a common cuff of tendon tissue that anchors into the head of the humerus and rotates the arm. (Copyright 2003 Nucleus Medical Art, all rights reserved. www.nucleusinc.com)

The shoulder is designed for maximum mobility. The main ball-and-socket joint of the shoulder can move in four directions, all of which come into play during the golf swing:

- Shoulder elevation lets you "Reach for the sky, partner."

- Internal rotation lets you scratch your back or fasten a bra strap.
- External rotation rotates the arm away from the body.
- The cross-arm position brings the arm and shoulder across the body.

It is interesting to compare the shoulder with the other major ball-and-socket joint in the body, the hip joint. Zillions of years of evolution have served to tweak the design of the shoulder and hip joints as humans evolved from four-legged to two-legged beings.

The hip joint remained a weight-bearing joint, where stability is necessary. Thus, the hip employs a very deep socket. But because the shoulder's job is no longer to walk but to position the hand in space, Mother Nature reengineered the shoulder to have a large ball and a very shallow socket. This design modification greatly increases joint mobility.

The increased mobility of the shoulder comes at a price, however. The shoulder is one of the most unstable joints in the body. It relies on secondary soft-tissue structures, such as a cartilage lip (called the labrum), to deepen and stabilize the joint. Furthermore, proper function and stability of the shoulder is dependent on the coordinated efforts of the numerous muscles of the shoulder, such as the rotator cuff (37).

Think of the hip joint as a pickup truck—simple and durable, but not high on performance. The shoulder is more like a sports car—more complicated, higher-performance, but also temperamental and more prone to breakdown due to its mechanical complexity.

The Shoulder and the Golf Swing

Dr. Frank Jobe, inventor of the "Tommy John" operation for the elbow and golf medicine expert, has conducted a series of research studies to reveal which muscles are most active at various phases of the golf swing. In one experiment, the shoulder muscle activity of seven right-handed professional golfers, none of whom had shoulder problems, was analyzed by inserting tiny wire electrodes into various shoulder muscles and recording the muscle activity of each player as they swung away with their golf clubs.

The studies yielded several important findings (38):

- The deltoid muscles of the right and left shoulders, instrumental in performing most overhead activities, were relatively inactive during all phases of the golf swing.
- Among the rotator cuff muscles, the subscapularis muscle, responsible for *internal rotation* of the shoulder and arm, was more active than any other throughout the swing.
- The rotator cuff muscles of the right side were just as active as those of the left (lead) shoulder.
- The pectoralis ("pecs") and latissimus ("lats") muscles showed marked activity during the downswing (acceleration) phase of the golf swing. Just as when throwing a baseball or serving in tennis, the pecs and lats provide major thrust. For the golfer, these muscles contribute significantly to club acceleration just prior to impact.

The results of the study bring into question the conventional wisdom among many golf gurus that the left shoulder provides more "drive" to the golf ball than does the right shoulder. Dr. Jobe and his colleagues concluded that *both* shoulders are equally important to the golf swing, and that greater distance can be achieved by exercising the rotator cuff, the pecs, and the lats on both sides (38).

A follow-up study that compared the shoulder muscle activity of healthy male and female professional golfers found that the shoulder muscle firing patterns of both sexes were strikingly similar (39).

The next logical study would be one to compare the shoulder-muscle firing pattern of the pro golfer with that of the amateur weekend hacker. The preceding chapter noted the significant differences in *spinal*-muscle firing patterns between pros and amateurs, so that might also be the case with the *shoulder* muscles. The shoulder-muscle firing pattern of the healthy pro, with his or her efficient "grooved" swing, may be significantly

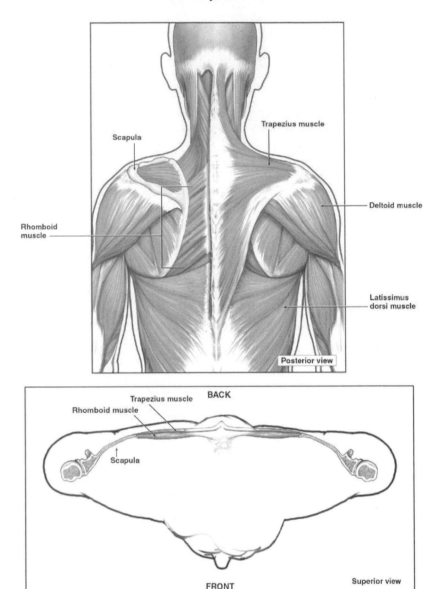

Figure 8-2. Important shoulder muscles. The golf swing requires the coordinated effort of many muscle groups. *Scapular lag* occurs when the muscles supporting the shoulder blade (scapula) are too weak to provide a stable base for the shoulder joint. Scapular lag can be a source of generalized shoulder pain throughout all phases of the golf swing. The most important scapular stabilizer muscles include the trapezius ("traps"), rhomboids, and serratus anterior (not pictured). The latissimus dorsi muscles ("lats") are critical to producing power during the downswing. (Copyright 2003 Nucleus Medical Art, all rights reserved. www.nucleusinc.com)

different from that of the hacker—or, from that of a golfer who is swinging with a shoulder injury.

Now, I'm all for the advancement of medical knowledge, but this is one study that I wouldn't be rushing to sign up for. Stick wires into my muscles just so you can tell me how screwed up my golf swing is? *No, thanks!*

The importance of muscle function and the golf swing is also seen in what is called "scapular lag." During the downswing, as the club head is building speed, the scapula (shoulder blade) must provide a stable "base" for the shoulder. But if the muscles supporting the scapula are weak, the scapula cannot provide a stable base. The resulting scapular lag, which can carry over through the downswing, impact, and follow-through phases, can make shoulder injury more likely (36)(77). The most important shoulder-blade stabilizing muscles include the trapezius ("traps"), levator scapulae, rhomboids, and serratus anterior muscles.

Shoulder Injuries and Treatment

Even though shoulder injuries in golf tend to be less common than injuries to other body parts, such as the lower back, swinging a golf club still places a significant amount of stress on the shoulder. A properly executed, and painless, golf swing requires the cooperation and synchronization of all of the seventeen muscles and four joints that make up the shoulder. If any of these muscles or joints is sufficiently out of whack, a painful swing can result.

Surveys have shown that both the frequency and type of shoulder injuries seen among players in the LPGA, PGA, and Senior PGA are similar (39). For both the professional and the amateur golfer, the likelihood of developing a shoulder injury appears to be due to several factors:

- Overuse (excessive play or practice)
- Improper swing technique
- Inadequate warm-up
- Poor strength and flexibility of the shoulder, arm, back, and legs
- Advancing age

It is important to note that there is a difference between pros and amateurs when it comes to two of the above factors. Pros aren't poorly conditioned, and they do warm up, so overuse and advancing age are more often problems for the professional golfer, whereas the amateur has all five factors to worry about.

Previous non-golf-related shoulder injuries can also adversely affect shoulder motion, strength, and stability—resulting in a painful shoulder on the golf course (36)(37).

Let's start by talking about the *aging shoulder.* Starting at about age thirty-five (Ouch! That used to sound so *old* to me!), several important changes that can affect shoulder performance begin to take place.

First, an age-related degeneration of the all-important rotator cuff tendon begins. As we age, the cuff can become thinner and develop tearing. Recall that a paltry blood supply often renders tendon tissue unable to repair itself adequately after injury. The rotator cuff tendon is no exception. These tears can be either all the way through the cuff (full thickness), or partway through the cuff (partial thickness). Dr. Frank Jobe reviewed the records of the many golfers he has treated for shoulder problems and determined that *injury to the rotator cuff accounts for the vast majority of golf-related shoulder injuries* (38).

Also, the small A-C joint, where the outer end of the collarbone meets the shoulder blade, tends to become arthritic with age. This can lead to pain at the A-C joint, particularly when the shoulder is placed in the cross-arm or overhead position. Bone spurs from the arthritic A-C joint might also press on the nearby rotator cuff tendon. As we get older, too, the normally thin layer of lubricating bursal tissue overlying the rotator cuff tendon can thicken and become inflamed, leading to shoulder bursitis.

Painful rotator cuff impingement can result from a weakened and degenerated rotator cuff combined with bone spurring and bursitis overlying the cuff. This is what my patient Carl has. In this case, as the arm is brought into the overhead position, the rotator cuff gets squashed (impinged) between the head of the humerus and the overlying shoulder blade. What is called "internal impingement" can also occur when the head of the humerus bangs up against the cartilage labrum inside the shoulder joint.

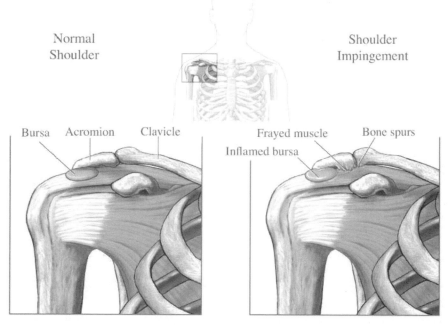

Normal Shoulder

Shoulder Impingement

Bursa   Acromion   Clavicle

Frayed muscle   Bone spurs

Inflamed bursa

Figure 8-3. Common shoulder problems. Shoulder problems frequently seen with increasing age among golfers include bursitis, arthritis and bone spurs at the A-C joint, and degeneration of the muscles and tendons of the rotator cuff. Shoulder *impingement* occurs when a weak and degenerated rotator cuff gets squashed (impinged) between the head of the humerus and the acromion portion of the shoulder blade. (Copyright 2003 Nucleus Medical Art, all rights reserved. www.nucleusinc.com)

All golfers—young or old, male or female, hacker or pro—are subject to developing shoulder problems *secondary to overuse*. A touring pro, for example, may put her shoulder through 2,000 revolutions a week. With each swing comes some degree of microscopic trauma to the important soft-tissue structures of the shoulder (rotator cuff, bursa, labrum, and shoulder joint capsule). Soft-tissue thickening and inflammation occur, resulting in shoulder pain and stiffness, and, with further injury, muscle weakness occurs. A vicious cycle ensues—the weakened and painful muscles are unable to do their part, which results in even more strain both on themselves on the surrounding shoulder tissues as additional golf shots are made.

Fortunately, the effects of mild to moderate rotator cuff tendonitis are reversible. Complete healing is possible if the golfer cuts back on repetitive overuse of the shoulder and follows up with a shoulder rehabilitation program. But when the rate of tissue injury exceeds the shoulder's capacity to heal and repair itself, microscopic injuries enlarge, and inflamed tissue can become irreversibly scarred. In this setting, more aggressive treatments, such as surgery, may be necessary (36)(37).

Another problem that is particularly common to the shoulder joint is *instability*. Recall that the mechanical design of the shoulder maximizes joint motion at the expense of stability. As the shoulder moves, there is a tendency for the head of the humerus to pop out of its socket. (For the record, a *subluxation* denotes when a joint pops out only partway, and *dislocation* describes a joint that has completely popped out.)

The only thing that keeps the ball centered in the socket is the complex array of stabilizing soft tissues (labrum, rotator cuff, and capsule of the shoulder joint). Injury to one of those structures, or weakness of the muscles of the shoulder, can allow the ball to sublux or dislocate out of the socket, resulting in further joint injury.

In general, shoulder instability tends to affect the younger golfer (less than thirty-five years old) (36). Shoulder stability can be enhanced through a rehabilitation program directed at strengthening and balancing the rotator cuff muscles. If instability problems persist, then various surgeries are available to "tighten" the supporting soft tissues to enhance shoulder stability.

Evaluating a patient with shoulder pain:

As with any clinical problem, the doctor evaluating the golfer with shoulder pain should begin with a complete history. The patient's age, handedness, occupation, and history of past shoulder injuries may all be important clues to the diagnosis.

- Pain is usually the main complaint. With the shoulder, pain is commonly felt with overhead activities or reaching behind the back. Pain when lying on the affected shoulder at night is also quite common. Shoulder problems frequently cause discomfort in the upper arm as well as in the shoulder itself. The pain can range from a mild aching to an excruciating stabbing pain.

- Pinpointing where the patient has pain and at what point in the golf swing can provide further clues to where the injury lies. For example, pain in the front of the left shoulder at the top of the backswing is typical of A-C joint arthritis pain (36).

- Numbness and tingling in the arm are not typical of shoulder injuries and may point to the presence of a problem elsewhere (a pinched nerve in the neck, for example).

- Shoulder range of motion is tested and compared with the opposite shoulder. Muscle strength, sensation, and reflexes are also checked and compared for each arm.

Special tests are also helpful in arriving at an accurate diagnosis:

- The *impingement test* is positive when the patient complains of pain as the examiner places the shoulder in the overhead position. Pain occurs because the injured rotator cuff is impinged between the head of the humerus and the overlying shoulder blade.

- The *cross-arm test* will be painful for patients suffering from A-C joint arthritis. Here, the arm is held out in front of and across the chest of the patient. In this position, the end of the collarbone is compressed against the upper part of the shoulder blade.

- The *apprehension test* is often positive in patients who have shoulder instability. Here, the examiner places the arm and shoulder in the same "cocked" position that one assumes when throwing a baseball. In patients with instability, an unpleasant feeling that the shoulder wants to "pop out" is elicited as the examiner further stresses the shoulder.

- *X-rays* of the shoulder are helpful for spotting abnormalities in the bones, such a joint space narrowing and bone spurring (signs of joint arthritis). Calcium deposits in the neighborhood of the rotator cuff (called "calcific tendonitis") may also be visible on X-rays.
- An *MRI scan* may be prescribed to visualize the soft-tissue, because most shoulder problems are not due to joint arthritis per se, but are the result of injury to the soft-tissue structures of the shoulder (rotator cuff, labrum, etc.) (36).

By putting all the pieces of the diagnostic puzzle together (history, physical exam, imaging tests), the physician can recommend an appropriate treatment plan. Many shoulder injuries can be successfully treated without surgery.

In his chapter on golf-related shoulder injuries in the book *Feeling up to Par,* Dr. James Andrews outlines an eight-phase program of medical treatment for the golfer who complains of a painful, weak, or stiff shoulder. This program, which emphasizes rehabilitation, can be employed once the physician has determined where the injury is in the shoulder (37):

- Phase I: Restricted activity, ice, and elimination of further trauma are initially employed to calm down the pain and inflammation of the shoulder injury.
- Phase II: Range-of-motion exercises are begun (as pain allows). The goal is to reestablish shoulder flexibility. Under the care of a therapist or trainer, the patient is encouraged to coax more and more motion from the injured shoulder.
- Phase III: Once mobility is regained, a progressive strengthening program using elastic bands and weights is begun. The goal is to strengthen and balance all the major shoulder muscle groups.
- Phase IV: A *limited* return to golf activity begins. Swing analysis by a local golf pro may expose faulty mechanics that brought on the shoulder injury (or perhaps made an injury worse). These swing deficiencies must be corrected

in order to prevent a recurrence of the problem once full play resumes.

- Phase V: Multiple-club practice is begun, with emphasis on increasing the number of swings per session as well as increasing distance. It is important to ensure that other important body areas—trunk, back, legs—are also restored to pre-injury conditioning.

- Phase VI: Return to full play. Just remember, if you stunk at golf before going through Phases I–V, you're still likely to stink now—but at least your shoulder won't hurt! And remember, consulting a pro along the way not only helps you to correct injury-producing swing flaws but also is sure to make you a better player as well. It is just as important to continue a maintenance program of rehabilitative exercises even after play has successfully resumed.

- Phase VII: If the above program does not result in a painless return to golf, cortisone injection into the shoulder, and with a repeat of phases I–VI, can be considered.

- Phase VIII: When symptoms of pain, weakness, and/or instability continue, despite a proper trial of rehab as outlined above, consideration can be given to surgery (37).

One thing I hear all the time from my patients, and not just golfers, goes something like this: "Doc, I work out at the gym four days a week and my arms are very strong already. Why do I need to go to a physical therapist to do exercises?"

This is a good question. The answer is that, although certain parts of the shoulder may be quite strong, a safe and painless golf swing requires the coordinated input from all, or at least most, of those seventeen shoulder muscles.

Muscle strength imbalance is a common cause of shoulder problems even among elite athletes (such as baseball pitchers), who are in also in top shape. A skilled therapist will be able to teach the golfer proper stretching and strengthening techniques for all the important golf muscles in the shoulder (rotator cuff, pecs, lats, shoulder blade stabilizers, and so on).

Shoulder Surgery

While many shoulder problems for the golfer can be successfully treated nonsurgically, certain structural injuries to the shoulder may remain painful despite a diligently applied rehab program. In this setting, surgery—particularly shoulder arthroscopy—may save the day. The development of arthroscopic surgical techniques has revolutionized the treatment of many common shoulder ailments and has allowed many golfers to get back to the game.

With arthroscopy, surgical trauma to the tissues is minimized by using tiny skin incisions, a fiber optic camera, and specialized instruments. The camera can be used to visualize all the major structures of the shoulder, including the bones, cartilage, ligaments, labrum, and rotator cuff. The shoulder joint can also be inspected for signs of arthritis and instability.

Many shoulder problems, including shoulder bursitis, impingement, A-C joint arthritis, and certain rotator cuff tears, can be addressed arthroscopically by a skilled surgeon. A few conditions, such as the repair of large rotator cuff tears, may require a larger (open) incision. To repair the cuff tear, the tendon tissue must be reattached to the humerus bone using a combination of sutures and various anchoring devices. Once the cuff has healed back to the bone, the rotator cuff muscles can be progressively rehabilitated.

Recall that the injury to the rotator cuff is believed to be the most frequent cause of shoulder pain affecting the golfer. Furthermore, rotator cuff tears may not respond to therapy alone and are a common reason for shoulder surgery. The golfer with a rotator cuff tear might well wonder if surgical repair will allow him to return to pain-free golf.

To date, only one study published in the medical literature has focused specifically on the effects of rotator cuff repair in the recreational golfer (48). In this study, twenty-nine recreational and regional tournament golfers were interviewed and examined for an average of three years after they had rotator cuff repair surgery. Results from this study shed some light on the nature of shoulder injuries and golf:

- The average patient age was sixty years old, the youngest golfer was thirty-nine, and the oldest was seventy-six. This makes sense, because we know that rotator cuff tears increase in frequency as the rotator cuff tendon weakens with age.
- Only one of the twenty-nine patients reported injuring a shoulder while playing golf. Twenty patients could not remember an injury at all, but reported a *gradual onset* of the symptoms. By the time surgery was scheduled, none of the twenty-nine patients was able to play golf, due to shoulder pain and weakness. This is evidence that, although golf may not be a frequent *cause* of rotator cuff tears, it can aggravate shoulder pain in the player who already has shoulder problems.
- The patients began strengthening exercises for the repaired rotator cuffs at about ten to twelve weeks after surgery. Chipping and putting were permitted at three months, while driving was delayed for four to five months after surgery. This illustrates a couple of points. First, rotator cuff repair surgery is a pretty big deal—it requires a great deal of patience and dedicated rehab to achieve a good result. Second, strenuous activities, such as playing golf, cannot be safely resumed until shoulder flexibility and strength have been regained.

Now for the best news:

- As many as 90 percent of the golfers were able to return to playing golf without pain. Furthermore, nearly nine out of ten were able to play at the same level they enjoyed before they hurt their shoulders. After recovering from their surgery, the golfers reported that their handicaps, driving distances, and number of rounds played per week were just about the same as before their injuries (48).

While more medical research is needed, the results of this study are encouraging. For the recreational golfer with a painful rotator cuff tear, the odds that a happy return to golf is possible look good.

Note: Golfers who have shoulder arthritis requiring joint replacement surgery should check out the chapter on Joint Replacement and the Golfer.

Advice from the Experts

Based on his many years of experience with golf-related shoulder injuries, Dr. Jobe has developed an algorithm to help golfers and doctors pinpoint the cause of a player's pain. He notes that most shoulder injuries occur to the *left* (lead) shoulder and that important information can be gained by asking the golfer two questions: Where does the shoulder hurt? and During what phase of the swing does it hurt? For example (36):

- At the top of the backswing, the left shoulder is placed in maximal cross-arm position. Pain felt in the front of the shoulder during this phase of the swing may be due to arthritis at the A-C joint (which gets compressed when the arm is held across the chest). Impingement of the head of the humerus against the cartilage labrum can also result in pain in the front of the left shoulder during this phase of the swing.

- Pain in the back of the left shoulder at the top of the backswing is likely due to tightness of the posterior shoulder capsule.

- Generalized shoulder pain during the downswing phase may be due to so-called scapular lag. If the scapular muscles are weak, the scapula cannot provide a stable base for the shoulder as the club accelerates. Generalized shoulder pain from scapular lag can also persist into the follow-through phase of the swing.

- During the follow-through phase, the left arm is horizontal to the ground and rotated away from the body (external rotation of the shoulder). Pain felt in the back of the shoulder during the follow-through may be due to injury to the posterior part of the cartilage labrum. Fraying of the rotator cuff tendon as it rubs against the labrum can also contribute to pain in the back of the shoulder during follow-through.

Parting Shots: The Shoulder

➤ Shoulder injuries occur as a result of several contributing factors: age, excessive play or repetitive practice, inadequate warm-up, and poor basic conditioning.

➤ A safe and efficient golf swing requires the coordination of many muscles from *both* shoulders. The left and right rotator cuffs, pecs, lats, and shoulder blade stabilizer muscles are particularly important. Exercises directed at these key muscle groups will improve swing efficiency and may decrease the risk of shoulder injury.

➤ Shoulder pain, weakness, and loss of mobility are signs of shoulder overuse and impending serious injury. Do not ignore these warning signs by continuing to play "through the pain."

➤ Nonsurgical care is successful in treating many shoulder problems. Rest, stretching and strengthening exercises, correction of swing mechanics, and a gradual return to golf activities is frequently enough to resolve many shoulder problems.

➤ Persistent shoulder problems are often successfully treated surgically. Rotator cuff repair, for example, allows many golfers to return to play with little or no pain. The majority of shoulder surgery can be performed arthroscopically, which usually allows a more rapid rehabilitation and return to sports.

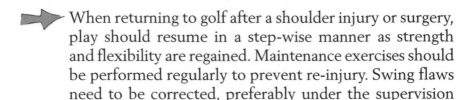 When returning to golf after a shoulder injury or surgery, play should resume in a step-wise manner as strength and flexibility are regained. Maintenance exercises should be performed regularly to prevent re-injury. Swing flaws need to be corrected, preferably under the supervision of a teaching pro.

Knee Injuries

Lorraine is a thirty-nine-year-old real estate agent. Every week, she and several friends get together for lunch and a round of golf. Lorraine usually walks the course for the exercise, but lately she's had to use a cart. It's her knee. About two months ago she felt a "pop" in her knee when swinging through a bunker shot. She didn't think much of it at first, but she tells me now that the knee feels swollen and tight after every round of golf. "It hurts me right here," she says, pointing to the inner half of her right knee. "It's like I get jabbed there every time I twist my knee. It hurts when I swing."

Lorraine's knee has bothered her off the golf course, too. "My knee wants to give out when I go down stairs, and I have to put a pillow between my knees at night. Otherwise, I can't sleep."

I explained to Lorraine that golf-induced injury to the knee is a relatively rare problem. Numerous surveys of amateur and professional players reveal that the knee accounts for less than 10 percent of all orthopedic golf injuries (4)(6)(32). Accordingly, knee pain in golfers has received much less attention in the medical literature than other more common problems, such as lower back or elbow injuries.

Although golf may not be the root cause of many *golf* injuries, playing golf, particularly for those of us who walk the course, may *aggravate* preexisting knee problems, such as cartilage tears or knee arthritis. This is particularly true for the older player.

Knee Anatomy 101

The knee joint is made up of four bones. The thighbone (femur) forms the upper part of the joint, and the shinbone (tibia) forms the lower part of the joint. A skinny bone (fibula) runs down the leg parallel to the shinbone and also forms part of the knee. The kneecap (patella) lives in the front of the knee joint.

The end of the thighbone, the top of the shinbone, and the back surface of the kneecap are each covered with a thin layer of smooth cartilage that provides a frictionless and protective surface for joint motion.

For the sake of simplicity, we can think of the knee joint as a simple hinge that bends (flexes) and straightens (extends). As the knee flexes and extends, the kneecap glides up and down in a cartilage-lined groove in the end of the thighbone.

The knee joint extends through the action of the quadriceps muscles in the front of the thigh. Knee flexion occurs courtesy of the hamstring muscles located in the back of the thigh. The quadriceps tendon, which connects the quadriceps muscles to the upper part of the kneecap, can tear (rupture) as a result of a sudden high-energy stress, such as a stumble down the stairs.

Quadriceps tendon rupture is not a common golf injury, but one case will live in golfing lore. Former President Bill Clinton (who, I understand, belongs in the Hackers Hall of Fame) ruptured his quadriceps tendon when he fell at the home of golf legend Greg Norman. Fortunately, alert Secret Service agents quickly subdued the offending stairway, and the President went on to a complete recovery and other pursuits.

In addition to the bones and muscles in the knee, several important soft-tissue structures give the joint *stability*.

The anterior and posterior cruciate ligaments (ACL and PCL) are thick crisscrossed ligaments that connect the thighbone and the shinbone and provide front-to-back stability. The ACL is frequently torn by violent twisting injuries, such as in football, soccer, or skiing—but *not* golf. The medial (inner) and lateral (outer) collateral ligaments (MCL and LCL, respectively) are designed to limit side-to-side motion of the knee as they tether the thighbone to the shinbone.

Inside the knee joint, situated between the thighbone and the shinbone, are two C-shaped cartilage structures called the medial (inner) and lateral (outer) meniscus. The function of these cartilage cushions is to spread out the weight-bearing stresses across the knee joint, thus avoiding excessive stress concentration to one small area. Injuries to these cartilages are among the most common causes of knee problems for both golfer and nongolfer alike. The medial meniscus is especially prone to tearing injuries.

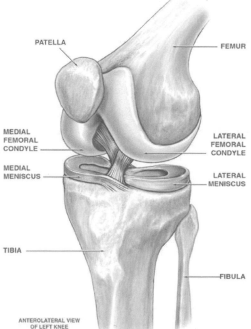

PATELLA

FEMUR

MEDIAL
FEMORAL
CONDYLE

LATERAL
FEMORAL
CONDYLE

MEDIAL
MENISCUS

LATERAL
MENISCUS

TIBIA

FIBULA

ANTEROLATERAL VIEW
OF LEFT KNEE

Figure 9-1. Basic knee anatomy. The thighbone (*femur*) forms the upper part of the knee joint, while the *tibia* and *fibula* form the lower part of the joint. The kneecap (*patella*) glides in a cartilage-lined groove in the end of the thighbone. Two C-shaped cartilage structures—the *medial* and *lateral meniscus*, act as cushions in the knee joint. (Copyright 2003 Nucleus Medical Art, all rights reserved. www.nucleusinc.com)

The Knee and the Golf Swing

Anyone who has attempted to set the clock on their VCR will agree that things are not always as simple as they first appear. For starters, the knee joint is not merely a simple hinge that swings like a hinge of a door. In fact, the knee is more like a sloppy hinge where things are a little loose, allowing motions and stresses that are more complex. Thus, during a golf swing the thighbone and shinbone not only flex and extend relative to each other; but also rotate (rotation stress), slide side-to-side (shear stress), and compress each other (compression stress).

The golf swing begins with the knees slightly bent and the golfer's body weight evenly distributed to both knees. During the backswing, the left knee and foot roll inward. Near the impact phase, body weight is shifted to the left (lead) knee. During the follow-through, the right knee moves to the left (as does the hip) as nearly all the body weight is shifted to the left leg (46).

Only a few published medical studies analyze the mechanics of the knee during the golf swing. One such study utilized video computer analysis of the swings of golfers of varying skill levels and made the following observations (54):

- The most stressful phase of the golf swing to the knee was the *downswing*.
- The skill level (handicap) of the golfer did not seem to affect the amount of stress placed on the knee during the swing.
- The stresses placed on the knee during the golf swing are not sufficiently high to result in frequent injury. This makes sense, because we already know from large-scale surveys of pro and amateur golfers that golf-induced knee injuries are not too common.
- However, the knee stresses caused by the golf swing *are* sufficiently high to be of concern to the golfer who is *rehabilitating* from a prior knee injury or knee surgery.

Naturally, first question that any devoted hacker will ask his orthopedist after surgery is, "Hey, Doc, when can I go out and play golf?" The next line is usually something like, "I *promise* I'll take it easy on the course."

The success of complex knee surgeries, such as anterior cruciate ligament repair, relies on adherence to a structured and step-wise rehabilitation protocol. Too much stress to the knee early after surgery can result in a disappointing re-injury. The authors of the above video computer analysis study calculated that certain stresses (particularly twisting/rotation) placed on the knee during the golf swing approach those seen during other stressful activities, such as running and cutting. The take-home message is that the golf swing may be too stressful for patients who are in the earlier stages of rehabilitation after certain types of knee surgery or injury. So if your doctor is not ready to let you perform running and cutting activities, then you probably are not ready for golf yet, either (54).

Evaluation and Treatment of Knee Injuries

In one published survey, golfers seeking care for knee pain at a busy orthopedic sports medicine practice were studied (47). These patients included both golfers who had actually injured their knees while playing golf as well as golfers who had preexisting knee problems that were aggravated by playing golf. Over the course of two years, thirty-five golfers were included in the study. The study noted:

- Most of the knee injuries occurred secondary to overuse, rather than as distinct traumatic injuries.
- Golfers of all ages had knee pain. The average age was fifty-six. The youngest golfer in the study was twenty-one, and the oldest golfer was seventy-three.
- Golfers of all abilities had knee pain. The handicaps of these golfers ranged from zero to 48 (the average handicap was 18). If nothing else, this proves there's at least one honest guy still out there in the world. Even Yours Truly doesn't have a handicap of 48! To me, anyone with guts enough to admit to having such a robust handicap deserves some sort of prize. Hmm, maybe we should get him a fishing pole—so the poor guy can take up a new hobby.
- The lead (left) knee and the trailing (right) knee were involved with equal frequency, while three golfers complained of pain in both knees.
- About half the thirty-five patients went on to have surgery.

After examining the patients and performing any necessary diagnostic tests (X-rays, MRIs, etc.), the study arrived at the following most common diagnoses:

Injury	Number of Cases
Torn medial meniscus	17/35
Knee arthritis (osteoarthritis)	10/35
Torn lateral meniscus	4/35
Kneecap pain (chondromalacia)	2/35

Most orthopedists would probably agree that the diagnoses listed above are the most common causes of knee pain among their golfing patients.

Let's look more closely at each of these common causes of knee pain, and the treatment options.

Torn Medial Meniscus

Because of the way most of people's knees are designed, the inner (medial) half of the knee takes on more stress than the outer half. Accordingly, the medial meniscus is injured more frequently than the lateral meniscus. The medial meniscus is often torn as a result of a twisting injury, such as a slip on a wet floor.

It is important to remember that not every meniscus tear occurs as a result of a single traumatic injury that the patient can distinctly recall. Some meniscus tears (the so-called *degenerative tears*) occur gradually, particularly in the older golfer. As we age, the meniscus cartilage undergoes changes in composition that reduce the pliability and resilience of the meniscus. Like an old rubber hose, the old meniscus is more susceptible to tearing than a young meniscus.

Evaluating a patient with a torn medial meniscus:

- The classic complaint from patients is pain localized to the inner half of the knee. Typically, the patient can pinpoint the painful spot with one fingertip.
- Clicking, popping, and a feeling that the knee is giving way are also common complaints. Twisting activities, such

as getting into and out of a car, can aggravate the pain, as can squatting.

- On physical exam, the most telling sign is tenderness along the inner joint line when the physician presses there with his thumb. Pain along the inner knee joint line is also elicited when the physician simultaneously twists the knee while flexing and extending the knee (a positive McMurray test).

- X-rays of the knee can be useful as an *initial* screening test (to rule out advanced arthritis, for example), but a meniscal tear cannot be seen on regular knee X-rays. This is because X-rays visualize only the bones—they do not see the soft tissues of the knee, such as the meniscus, tendons, or ligaments.

- An MRI scan is the test of choice in order to "see" a torn meniscus. It can provide highly accurate images of all the major soft-tissue structures of the knee. The safe and painless MRI procedure has revolutionized medicine over the past twenty years.

It's important to note that not all medial meniscus tears are painful. A couple of years ago, I had a nagging pain on the outer side of my right knee. To my surprise, an MRI revealed a tear of my medial meniscus, even though I'd never had pain in my inner knee. With time, the pain went away, but I've never treated my meniscus tear—though I am sure it's still lurking in there.

This brings up an important point that I constantly stress to my patients: Doctors treat *people*, not X-rays and MRIs. To me, what counts most is what a patient *feels*, not what the fancy tests show. Reducing pain, increasing function, and improving quality of life are the objectives of the good orthopedist.

Meniscus cartilage has a very poor capacity to heal once it is torn, so the best one can hope for is that the *symptoms* go away—and sometimes, with a little luck, they do. Several treatment options are available, once a torn medial meniscus is diagnosed:

Simple measures, such as rest, NSAID medication, or a cortisone injection, may help decrease the discomfort.

Knee arthroscopy has become the standard treatment for medial meniscus tears that cause ongoing and disabling pain. Here, the surgeon is able to enter the knee through a couple of small incisions and see the meniscus tear (as well as the rest of the inside of the knee) using a fiber optic camera and a TV screen. The meniscus tear is usually not repairable—remember, meniscus cartilage is lousy at healing. Instead, the torn portion of the meniscus is removed using specialized miniature operating instruments. The whole procedure usually takes less than an hour, and patients are sent home the same day. After arthroscopy, patients are usually getting around on the knee pretty well within a few weeks, and may be able to return to golf within a couple of months.

Torn Lateral Meniscus

The lateral meniscus is the twin of the medial meniscus. It sits in the outer (lateral) space between the thighbone and the shinbone. Pretty much everything I said about medial meniscus tears applies to lateral meniscus tears, except that the pain is located on the outer half of the knee. Lateral meniscus tears are less common than medial meniscus tears, but the treatment is the same. For persistently painful tears, arthroscopy is an effective treatment.

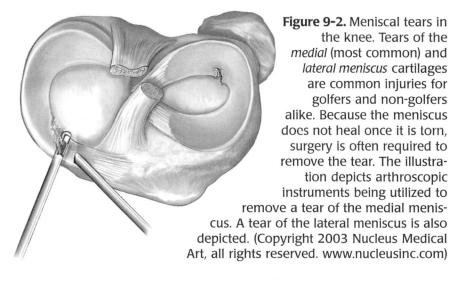

Figure 9-2. Meniscal tears in the knee. Tears of the *medial* (most common) and *lateral meniscus* cartilages are common injuries for golfers and non-golfers alike. Because the meniscus does not heal once it is torn, surgery is often required to remove the tear. The illustration depicts arthroscopic instruments being utilized to remove a tear of the medial meniscus. A tear of the lateral meniscus is also depicted. (Copyright 2003 Nucleus Medical Art, all rights reserved. www.nucleusinc.com)

Knee Arthritis (Osteoarthritis)

The medical term "arthritis" is a rather vague and general term referring to a disease process involving a joint. "Osteoarthritis" refers to an *age-related* wear-and-tear degeneration of a joint. Symptoms of knee arthritis generally develop gradually.

Initially, in the knee, the thin layer of cartilage that lines the end of the thighbone, the top of the shinbone, and the back of the kneecap softens. With further injury, the cartilage can crack and flake away, leaving exposed areas of bone with no cushion. This causes painful bone-on-bone contact between the joint surfaces, and spikes and ridges of new bone ("bone spurs") may form along areas of bone contact. The medial and lateral meniscus can also degenerate and tear, causing more pain. With very advanced arthritis, a bow-legged or knock-kneed deformity can develop over time.

(For a more complete discussion of osteoarthritis, please refer to the chapter on Joint Replacement and the Golfer.)

Evaluating a patient with knee arthritis:

- Pain—which can range from an annoying ache to incapacitating pain that interfere with daily activities, such as walking or sleeping—is the main complaint.
- Taking a medical history can rule out other common causes of knee arthritis, such as rheumatoid arthritis.
- On physical examination, the arthritic knee is typically swollen, stiff, and tender to touch. Joint motion, which is normally smooth and painless, is replaced with clicking and crunching due to the loss of cartilage lining the bones.
- X-rays of the knees, particularly those taken standing, reveal a narrowing of the space between the thighbone and shinbone, as well as bone spurring.

The physician treating a patient with arthritis of the knee has numerous options.

Initially, nonsurgical treatment is attempted:

- Rest and modification of activities can help. For instance, a golfer with knee arthritis might be happier at the end of the day if he used a cart instead of walking the course.

- Weight loss. Every pound lost is one less pound the arthritic knee has to bear.
- NSAID medication, which can significantly reduce the symptoms of knee arthritis pain, swelling, and stiffness.
- Dietary supplements, such as glucosamine and chondroitin, which are believed to have a cartilage-sparing effect on arthritic joints.
- Physical therapy, to help restore joint motion and strength.
- Cortisone injections (used sparingly) into the knee joint, for temporary relief of joint pain.
- Injection of lubricating fluid into the knee (viscosupplementation). Here, a thick synthetic fluid (derived from animal cartilage) is injected into the knee joint to replace the normal lubricating and cushioning fluid that is lost as the knee becomes arthritic.
- Bracing the arthritic knee to provide support and symptom relief.

Surgery is reserved for patients with debilitating symptoms from knee arthritis who fail to get relief from nonsurgical treatment:

- Knee arthroscopy has a limited role in the treatment of knee arthritis. Symptoms can sometimes improve if an arthritic knee is "cleaned out" arthroscopically. However, arthroscopic surgery cannot *undo* arthritis. The patient and doctor must have realistic expectations about what will be achieved with arthroscopy alone. In general, the more advanced the arthritis, the less likely that an arthroscopy will be a home-run.
- The ultimate treatment for painful knee arthritis is a surgical procedure called *total knee replacement*. Here, the arthritic joint surfaces are replaced with a prosthesis made of metal and plastic. Evidence gathered so far from surgeons and patients indicates that patients can safely resume golf after total knee replacement, and that playing golf does not appear to increase the rate of complications after surgery (17)(18)(20). (See the chapter on Joint Replacement and the Golfer for a more complete discussion.)

Kneecap Pain (Chondromalacia)

As we bend and straighten a knee, the kneecap (patella) glides up and down in a cartilage-lined groove in the end of the thighbone. Many people who suffer from kneecap pain have misalignment of the kneecap (particularly females).

If the kneecap is off-center in its groove, portions of the cartilage on the back surface of the kneecap can become injured. Initially, the cartilage becomes softened (chondro = cartilage; malacia = softening). With further injury, cracking and flaking of the cartilage can occur, resulting in painful bone-on-bone contact between the thighbone and the kneecap. Direct-blow injuries to the front of the knee (such as a fall onto the flexed knee, or a dashboard injury during a car accident) can injure the kneecap cartilage as well.

Evaluating a patient with kneecap pain:

- Patients typically report a deep-seated achy sensation in the front of the knee. Walking (especially up and down hills or stairs), squatting, and kneeling usually make the discomfort worse.

- Sitting with the knee bent for a long time will also bring on that annoying ache. It's not unusual for patients with kneecap pain to choose the seat at the end of the row when in a movie theater. This makes it possible for them to straighten the leg in the aisle periodically to minimize the ache from the kneecap (a positive "movie theater sign"). Patients with kneecap pain who are new to my practice think I'm some sort of Amazing Kreskin when I correctly guess where they prefer to sit in the movie theater.

- On physical exam, patients with kneecap pain may exhibit crunching and grinding as the kneecap glides up and down. Pain is provoked as the examiner presses the kneecap into the thighbone (a positive "patella grind test").

Kneecap pain, in general, is difficult to treat and almost impossible to make go away completely.

- Physical therapy is a popular first line of treatment. The emphasis is on strengthening the quadriceps muscles in the thigh, which can help correct the misalignment of the kneecap. Stretching of the hamstrings and Achilles tendon is also emphasized (46).
- Knee bracing and shoe orthotics can also help alleviate kneecap pain.
- NSAID medication can help take the edge off the discomfort.
- In rare cases, surgery is available to treat patients with severe kneecap pain.

Advice from the Experts

Dr. Gary Guten, the orthopedic surgeon who authored the survey of the thirty-five golfers with knee problems, has several general recommendations for golfers with knee problems (47).

Pregame Preparation and Equipment Selection

- Get help from a golf pro, particularly with the assistance of video teaching techniques, to correct swing imperfections that may be contributing to knee pain.
- Rest, or playing or practicing less frequently, may be all that it takes for knee pain to improve. I might add that using a cart, rather than schlepping the course on foot, should also minimize knee pain. Rest is a recurring theme throughout this book, and it is one that is difficult to impress on the often-hardheaded golfer. For most of us, *golf* is our rest. We don't like being told that we should play less golf in order to let our injured bodies to heal.
- Use short irons. Dr. Guten's patients reported that their knee pain was especially bad on long-distance shots—those hit with a driver, a 3-wood, or long irons (2 through 6 irons). Using the short irons (7, 8, 9, and the wedges) seemed to cause less strain on the knees and less pain. It could be that the twisting motions of the full golf swing cause more stress on the knees than the shorter swing

utilized when playing with the short irons. So, golfers recovering from a knee injury, or knee surgery, might be better off easing back into golf by sticking to the short irons. (Hey, why not go check out that executive par-3 course you've always wanted to try?). If these short shots do not cause any knee pain, then a progression to longer clubs and longer swings can be attempted.

- Play without spiked shoes. Dr. Guten's patients reported that they had less knee pain if they played without spiked shoes. It might be that the golfer who knows that he or she isn't "anchored" to the ground with spiked shoes may tend to swing with less intensity, and thereby put less strain on the knees (47). However, another published study determined that shoe type (spiked versus spikeless) did not significantly affect the amount of stress transmitted to the knees during the golf swing (54). This study was conducted under simulated conditions while hitting from rubber mats. The authors did note that shoe type may affect knee stress levels under real playing conditions (on real turf). Further studies are needed to settle this issue.
- Improve conditioning. By increasing the strength and flexibility of the upper body, the golfer with knee problems will rely less on the legs.

The Address and the Backswing

- Distribute body weight equally on both legs, to help minimize stress on the knees. Some golf schools advocate that golfers sway during their swing and release their neck and back to reduce pain in these areas, but swaying may place additional stress on the left knee. Conversely, hitting with too much weight on the back foot may place too much stress on a sore right knee.
- Adopt a swing pattern that is more upright, with the knees not bent as much as usual. Golfers playing on sore knees naturally tend to use this more upright swing position.

Again, distributing the weight evenly to both legs will also equalize the stress placed on the knees.

- Experiment with foot position during the swing, to decrease knee pain. For example, turning the feet slightly *outward* may reduce the stress of turning on the knee.

Parting Shots: The Knee

Knee injuries *caused* by golf are relatively uncommon. However, knee problems are very common overall, particularly for the older golfer, and playing golf may aggravate these injuries.

Although stresses placed on the knee during the golf swing are not high enough to *cause* many injuries, the stresses are high enough to be of concern to the player who is recovering from knee surgery or a knee injury. In such a situation, the golfer should return to play under a doctor's supervision.

Effective treatments for the most common knee problems, including cartilage tears and knee arthritis, are available.

Most patients can safely return to playing golf after total knee replacement surgery.

The Golf
Warm-Up

If you've been paying any attention at all, you've noticed a recurring theme in this book. Golf injuries among amateurs are caused by a combination of factors, including overuse (excessive play or repetitive practice), poor conditioning, faulty swing technique, *and improper warm-up*. Now, I have a confession to make. While I have gone to great lengths scour the medical literature to make this book as scientifically accurate as possible, I have to admit that there is not a single article that conclusively links improper warm-up with an increased risk of golf injury (62). Such studies simply do not exist.

That said, you should know that it is the opinion of every golf expert I have read that there *is* a direct link between a good warm-up and injury prevention. And any serious athlete will tell you the same thing. To see for yourself, go to a professional ballpark two hours before the game. The players are all out there—doing calisthenics, stretching, and wind sprints. Better yet, ask any local golf pro. You will surely learn that the pros spend a considerable amount of time warming up before they practice or play. Unfortunately, most recreational golfers think that the first three holes of their round *is* the warm-up.

Sports physiologists define *the warm-up* as a "period of preparatory exercise undertaken to enhance subsequent competition or training performance" (62). Sports physicians and athletes alike believe that warm-up activities not only improve subsequent performance but also reduce the risk of injury.

Numerous laboratory studies have shown that "warm" muscles have several advantages over "cold" muscles. Specifically, a warm muscle exhibits more rapid impulse conduction and produces more force. Furthermore, increased muscle temperature increases the efficiency of muscular contraction (more bang for the energy buck, so to speak). Finally, a warm muscle is more elastic (extensible) than a cold muscle. An increase in temperature also has beneficial effects on the elasticity and efficiency of tendons and ligaments.

Muscles get warm in two different ways. First, a contracting muscle generates its own heat energy. Second, the increased blood flow delivered to an actively working muscle also increases the temperature of that muscle (44).

The joints also benefit from the warm-up routine due to increases in joint motion and the circulation of joint lubricating fluid.

Stretching is another important component of the sports warm-up. Stretching increases muscle and tendon flexibility. A stretched muscle or tendon unit can store more energy and work more efficiently than a stiff muscle or tendon. In addition, it is believed that a stretched muscle or tendon is at lower risk for injury than a stiff muscle or tendon (44).

Stretching is actually most beneficial *after* the muscles are warmed up—not before. A warm muscle can be stretched more with less risk of injury (69).

Now, let's redefine the golf warm-up in plain English. A good golf warm-up includes a period of exercise to get the heart going and warm up the muscles, followed by stretching of the "golf muscles." Once the golfer is warmed and stretched, he or she can then begin swinging the club with a *gradual* progression in swing motion and intensity.

The initial exercise part of the warm-up can include any light aerobic activity. Brisk walking, jogging, or calisthenics (for example, jumping jacks) will all do the trick. The aerobic activity chosen should be appropriate for the golfer's age and level of conditioning. A good rule of thumb to use is the "sweat rule"—if you've done enough brisk walking, jogging, or calisthenics to break a light sweat, you are ready to proceed with the rest of the warm-up.

Stretches can be either *static* (where the muscle or joint is held in a set position) or dynamic (where the muscle or joint is moved through a wide range of motion). A combination of both types of stretches is recommended. There are many "golf muscles" to stretch—hands, wrists, forearms, shoulders, lower back, chest, trunk, groin, and legs all need attention (62).

Now that we know what a good warm-up is, we can ask whether any of we recreational golfers actually *do warm up* in the real world. That very question was at the center of one of my favorite golf research studies, published in the *British Journal of Sports Medicine.*

For this study, two undercover observers staked out three golfing venues in Australia: a private golf club, a public course, and a driving range. (I wonder whether they wore those cool hats with one side flipped up, as if they were stalking dangerous prey in the outback!) They secretly observed and recorded all warm-up activities of randomly selected adult golfers before they hit their first ball. Overall, more than 1,000 golfers (882 men and 188 women) were observed, and the results are not pretty (62):

- Barely half (54 percent) of the golfers performed any sort of warm-up activity before beginning play.
- Of those who did do some sort of warm-up, the most commonly observed routine consisted solely of air swings at or just before the first tee. To make things worse, the average number of air swings taken was a measly two.
- Only about one in ten golfers (12 percent) did any sort of stretching before hitting away. The average number of stretches performed by those who did stretch was a paltry one.
- None of the golfers was observed performing any sort of aerobic warm-up exercise.

The authors concluded that the warm-up habits of the amateur golfer are woefully inadequate. Less than 3 percent of the golfers were judged to have even approached what is considered to be a proper golf warm-up.

Now, did these researchers just happen to stumble on 1,000 particularly lazy golfers, or are we pretty much *all* guilty of neglecting to warm up adequately? I suspect the latter is true, but don't wait for this study to be repeated in America—too dangerous. Any researcher caught spying on golfers from the bushes is likely to end up with a putter stuck up his nose—or worse.

The typical amateur warm-up, or lack thereof, is in stark contrast to the pregame routine of the typical pro. Professionals do not jump from the clubhouse to the tee without warming up—they know that to do so would put them at increased risk for injury. They also know that their performance on the course would suffer without a proper warm-up.

After the muscles have been warmed and stretched, the pro will then begin swinging and hitting balls. The key is to gradually increase the length and intensity of the swings to allow the muscles and tendons a chance to continue to warm up and adapt. Putting and short pitches are typically practiced first, followed by use of lower-loft clubs. The driver (the club requiring the most forceful and strenuous swing) is taken out of the bag only after the golfer is fully "warm" (31).

Face it—you and I do the exact opposite. At the range, we take out our shiny titanium-platinum-molybdenum alloy Widowmaker III driver *first*. We launch a few dozen shots with that baby—*then* we take out the short clubs at the end. Putting? Who practices *putting?*

The Golf Warm-Up—A Pro's Perspective

Tom Nieporte is a highly respected golf teacher and has been the head teaching pro at Winged Foot Golf Club (site of the 1984 U.S. Open and the 1998 PGA Championship) for the past twenty-five years. As a touring pro, Tom competed thirteen times in both the U.S. Open and the PGA Championship. He has three Tour victories to his credit, including the 1967 Bob Hope Desert

Classic. Tom is also a master of the mental aspects of the game, having co-written the book *Mind Over Golf* (see Recommended Reading at the end of the book).

Tom has played with the best at the highest competitive level. He understands the importance of a proper warm-up—not only for the professional golfer, but for the recreational player as well. Tom has the following wise words of experience to share with us about warming up:

> *There is no more rewarding feeling than hitting a ball in the center of the club face and seeing it soar through the air. Top professionals have a secret that helps them hit great shots regularly. They realize their body is their livelihood—and they take good care of it like a mechanic tunes a Rolls-Royce. They know that muscle strains and spasms can lead to injuries that can shorten their careers.*
>
> *While playing on the Tour, I have seen pros forced to withdraw from many tournaments because of back, shoulder, elbow, wrist, neck, and hand injuries. With all its torque, the golf swing is strenuous exercise. These days, after coming off the eighteenth green, most touring pros will practice, and then finish their day in the fitness trailer where highly-skilled physical therapists work to keep them in top condition. I wish we had such facilities when I was playing the Tour—and I am almost certain that such legends as Ben Hogan, Byron Nelson, and Sam Snead could have benefited from the attention today's pros receive.*
>
> *Gary Player realized something early. He was a pacesetter for physical conditioning in order to play better golf. He had very few injuries during his successful career that continues today.*
>
> *When I was competing on the Tour—and it continues today—pros arrived at the course early so they could have plenty of time to warm-up. Sometimes it isn't possible. Players can be delayed by traffic, a flat tire, a broken*

alarm clock, or other problems. Without a chance to stop at the range, they still somehow managed to loosen up with stretches and practice swings. There were times that happened to me. Thank goodness, I wasn't late very often.

The next time you go to a golf tournament, visit the range and watch the touring pros warm up. Like many players alongside me on the range, I would follow a routine. After starting a few short shots with the wedge, I'd hit a few shots with my odd-numbered irons. The next day, I might use the even-numbered irons. I'd finish by hitting at least five to ten drives before going to the putting green to chip, hit a few sand shots, and putt for at least fifteen minutes. My goal was clear—to tune my body to meet the competitive challenge ahead.

In virtually all professional sports, top athletes are sure to exercise properly so they can excel on the course or in the arena. They want to perform at the highest level their bodies will allow. You can do that too by taking a tip from the pros. Warm up the way the top athletes do.

We amateurs should take a lesson from this seasoned golf master. Okay, so our bodies may be more like a Yugo than a Rolls-Royce. And we may be playing for only a few beers, not a few hundred thousand dollars. Nonetheless, we must get into the habit of treating our bodies properly in order to maximize performance and prevent injury.

Doctor Divot's Golf Warm-Up

There are four facets to the optimum golf warm-up:

- Time
- Aerobic exercise
- Stretching
- Progressive swinging

Time

In order to get into the habit of warming up before golfing, you must first allow yourself the *time* to do it. Rushing frantically from the parking lot to the tee is a great way to ruin the start of what should be a relaxing day. Being in a hurry is also a great excuse for not doing a proper warm-up. Get into the habit of leaving the house or office twenty minutes or so earlier than you are accustomed. By avoiding that rushed feeling, you can spend time preparing to be both mentally and physically ready to play. It will be time well spent, I promise.

Aerobic Exercise

Once at the course, you should start with a five minute aerobic "sweat breaker." Briskly walking around the parking lot, jogging, running in place, or jumping jacks (my favorite, because it gets the shoulders going as well) will all suffice. Choose whatever is your own favorite. Don't worry about appearing odd, either—just look down at those ridiculous looking golf saddle shoes your playing partner is wearing, and you won't feel so silly after all. Remember, too, to **choose an activity that is appropriate for your age and level of conditioning. If you have any questions, consult your doctor first.** Nobody wants a sweat-breaker to turn into a heart-breaker.

Stretching

I prefer a "head-to-toe" approach to stretching, because it provides a way for me to remember to include all the major muscle groups in sequence. Hold each stretch for fifteen to twenty seconds. Avoid stretching beyond the point of pain, and never bounce to stretch. Stretch one side of the body, then the other. Repeat the stretches three or four times for each side.

Figure 10-1A.
Neck rotation.

Neck rotation: Turn your head all the way to the left and hold. You can add a little more stretch by pushing your chin with your fingertips. Repeat for the right side.

Figure 10-1B.
Neck flexion.

Neck flexion: Pretend you are looking at a spot of mustard on your shirt. Flex your neck to bring your chin as close to your chest as you can go and hold.

Figure 10-1C.
Lateral neck stretch.

Lateral neck stretch: Looking straight ahead, cock your head to the left as if you were trying to bring your left ear to your shoulder (don't cheat by shrugging your shoulder up to meet your ear). Repeat for the right side.

Figure 10-1D.
Posterior shoulder stretch.

Posterior shoulder stretch: Pretend you have an itch between your shoulder blades. Hold your left arm across your body and grab the back of your left elbow with your right hand. Pull the left elbow in as far as you can so that your left fingertips can reach your upper back. Repeat for the right shoulder.

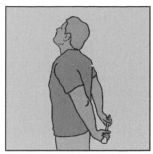

Anterior shoulder and chest stretch:
Hold a club with both hands behind
your back, elbows extended. Now stick
out your chest while you raise the club
back away from your body and hold.

Figure 10-1E. Anterior
shoulder/chest stretch.

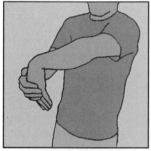

Figure 10-1F.
Forearm/wrist flexion.

Forearm and wrist stretch: Hold you left
arm out in front of you with your elbow
locked straight. Now take your right
hand and bend (flex) your left wrist and
hand as far down as they will go and hold
(remember to keep your elbow straight).
Now repeat the stretch but this time
turn your left palm up and use your right
hand to extend the left wrist as far as
they will go. Repeat for the right side.
This exercise loosens the wrists and also
prevents tennis elbow and golfer's elbow so don't skimp here.

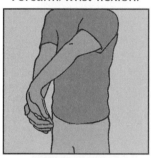

Figure 10-1G.
Forearm/wrist extension.

Lateral back stretch: Hold a club with
both hands over your head. Keeping
your pelvis steady, bend as far as you can
to the left and hold. Slowly return to
the upright position and repeat to the
right side.

Figure 10-1H.
Lateral back stretch.

Toe touch: This stretches the lower back. Stand with your feet shoulder-width apart. Slowly bend forward at the waist and try to touch your toes. There is a huge degree of variation among people regarding how far they can go, so don't feel bad if you can't reach all the way to your toes. Remember not to bounce. If you have a bad back you can sit on a bench and lean over to touch your toes instead.

Figure 10-1I.
Toe-touch.

Figure 10-1J. Lower back/trunk rotation.

Lower back / trunk rotation: I prefer to do this one sitting down. You can use the golf cart seat or a bench. Pretend you're driving to the Grand Canyon while your kids have been arguing in the back seat for six hours straight and you are going to now yell at them. Keeping your hips facing forward, rotate your body all the way to the left, look over your shoulder and hold. If you like, you can grab hold of the back of the bench or seat. Repeat for the right side. Saying "Do I have to stop this car?" is optional.

Hamstring stretch: Stand upright and place your left foot on the golf cart or bench. Now bend forward at the waist while keeping your back straight. Repeat for the right side.

Figure 10-1K.
Hamstring stretch.

Quads stretch: Pretend you stepped in some chewing gum and you are checking the bottom of your shoe. Stand with your feet close together. Now grab your left ankle behind you and flex your knee as far as it will go and hold (your left heel should hit your buttocks). Repeat for the right side. If necessary, hold on to the golf cart or a tree for balance. To get the most out of this stretch, keep the trunk straight and avoid leaning forward.

Figure 10-1L.
Quads stretch.

Figure 10-1M.
Calf stretch.
(Illustrations 10-1 A-M
by Moki Kokoris)

Calf stretch: Pretend you are a sword fighter about to thrust at your opponent. Stand with your right foot about eighteen inches in front of your left foot. Keep your left heel on the ground as you lean forward, flexing your right knee as you go. You will feel a stretch in your left calf muscles. Repeat for the right side. If necessary, you can hold on to the golf cart or a tree for balance as you lean forward.

Progressive Swinging

So far you've given yourself ample time, broken a sweat with your aerobic routine, and performed a leisurely head-to-toe stretch. Now you are ready to pick up a club and start swinging.

Start with a sand or lob wedge by first taking a few half and three-quarter swings before working up to full swings. Next, go through your bag using the same pattern of half to full swings with each of your even- or odd-numbered irons, starting with the highest number. Work your way down to the 3 or 4 iron.

Next come the woods. Because they require an even more strenuous swing than the irons, make sure you are completely warmed and stretched. As a final back stretcher before hitting the big boys, I like to hold a wood behind my back, locking my elbows around the club shaft, and gently rotate from one side to the other through my lower back. Hit your 7 wood a few times first, then the 5 and 3 woods. Finish with your driver. Next, after crushing one down the middle of the practice range, turn to your playing partner (who is standing in slack-jawed astonishment at your newfound dedication to your body's well-being) and say, "Let's go, Sucker!"

For those of you who play at courses without practice ranges, it's still a good idea to go through your clubs in a step-wise manner, taking half and then full phantom swings instead of actually hitting balls. Your muscles, tendons, and ligaments will still benefit from the progressive workout you are giving them. Besides, phantom swings are always perfect—aren't they?

The question of when to practice putting and chipping is open for debate. Because these swings are least stressful to the body, it makes sense to do them first. However, some folks might argue that these shots are the most stressful on the brain and should be practiced last to be ready for battle. Whichever system works best for you is fine with me.

Now you're ready to go get 'em, Ace!

Conditioning and Preventive Exercises for Golf

Have you ever overheard someone in the clubhouse locker room say "I don't work out because if I bulk up too much I'll lose my flexibility and my golf swing will suffer"? Personally, I was never clever enough to come up with an excuse like that not to exercise—I'm just plain lazy. Whatever may be your excuses for not getting into shape, the fear of losing flexibility and of decreased golf performance should not be among them. It is a myth that golf performance will suffer if a player engages in a strength-training program (65).

One of the recurring themes of this book is that swinging a golf club is a demanding sports activity. Okay, so it doesn't require the endurance of running a marathon or the brute strength of bench pressing 400 pounds. But, during the two seconds it takes to perform a golf swing we accelerate the club head to speeds of 100 miles an hour or more—which is pretty macho stuff when you think about it.

So, while the golf swing may not require great strength, it does demand rapid, coordinated, and cooperative movement from many muscle groups. We have seen in previous chapters that the golf swing stresses certain muscle groups to near all-out capacity (the spinal and trunk muscles, for example). Things really start to add up when you consider that an average round of golf involves about fifty to sixty swings (not including prac-

149

tice swings and putts) and that walking the course amounts to a five-mile walk that burns almost 1,000 calories (61).

Another comment frequently heard in the locker room is "I play golf so often that I don't need extra conditioning." Wrong. The concept of "playing oneself into shape" is another stubborn myth that sports medicine experts have had trouble putting to rest among recreational golfers (61). The modern-day golf pro is proof of the value of conditioning in golf. Although these men and women play more rounds in a year than most of us will in a lifetime, conditioning has been accepted as a necessary and fundamental part of the game. In fact, the PGA provides a fitness trailer staffed with therapists that tours along with the players. Things have come a long way since the 1960s, when Gary Player was considered a ground-breaker for advocating off-season conditioning (69).

Admittedly, no one is maintaining that the gal or guy who plays a few rounds of golf a month needs to hit the gym the same way that Tiger Woods is known for. That said, it is a widely held conviction among golf medicine experts that a flexible and strong musculoskeletal system is better protected from the excessive forces of the golf swing than a poorly conditioned body is (61).

Golf Fitness

The key components to golf fitness, are:
- Strength
- Flexibility
- Aerobic conditioning

Strength

In the golf swing, muscle force generates club head speed, and club head speed is what sends the ball flying. During the swing, muscle power is transferred from the legs through the body to the club head.

What, then, are the key "golf muscles" that we should be concerned with? Scientific research on the golf swing has taught us that there are *lots* of important golf muscles, some of the most important of which are (38)(61):

- The rotator cuff muscles of the shoulder, both right and left
- The scapular stabilizing muscles, including the trapezius, the levator scapulae, the rhomboids, and the serratus anterior muscles—all of which are important for prevention of what is called "scapular lag."
- The pectoral and latissimus muscles—which are key in developing power during the downswing
- The erector spinae and abdominal oblique muscles of the trunk, which are most active during the initiation of the forward swing and during the acceleration phase
- The gluteal and hamstring muscles of the hips and thighs, the contributions of which to the power of the golf swing are often overlooked
- The forearm flexor and extensor muscles, which provide a firm grip and stabilize the club as it impacts the ball

Flexibility

We are all familiar with the red line on the upper portion of our car's tachometer gauge. It's there to warn us that if we push the engine beyond its stress tolerance bad things will happen. Our muscles and joints have limits too. If we push them beyond their stress tolerances, bad things (like strains and sprains) will happen. But *flexibility training* stretches our muscles, ligaments, and tendons in a *controlled, gradual, and progressive way*. The net result, over time, is that the golf swing no longer stresses our muscles and joints to their extreme limits of motion. It's almost as if we nudge that red line on the tachometer farther and farther.

The golf swing is particularly tough on the spine and the trunk. Recall how the "modern" golf swing combines a large shoulder turn with a restricted hip turn to store energy in the spine and trunk like a giant coiled spring. Researchers have noted that trunk flexibility is a key difference between the professional golfer and the amateur. Some experts believe that improving trunk mobility is the most important component of a successful golf conditioning program. Improving trunk and spine flexibility in the recreational golfer will likely result both in improved swing performance and in decreased risk of injury (60)(61).

Some important concepts to keep in mind regarding stretching exercises include (69):

- Stretches are best performed after muscles and tendons have been warmed up by some preliminary aerobic exercises (for example, five to ten minutes of light calisthenics, jogging, and brisk walking).
- Stretches should be done slowly and held for about 15 to 20 seconds. Avoid bouncing, which can lead to injury. Try stretching to the limit of the muscle or joint without inducing actual pain or forcing the joint beyond its normal range of motion.
- Don't go crazy all at once. Instead, go slowly and try to add a little more stretch each session.

Aerobic Conditioning

By definition, an aerobic activity is any exercise that increases the heart rate to 75 percent of a predicted maximum and keeps it there for at least twenty minutes, three times a week. The "target" heart rate varies depending on the athlete's age. Popular aerobic activities include brisk walking, jogging, biking, and swimming (61)(66).

Research studies have classified playing a round of golf—walking—as a low-to-moderate-intensity exercise that will increase or maintain aerobic fitness in middle-aged players (72). So, while playing golf won't get you in shape to climb Mount Everest, it is certainly better for you than sitting around the house.

Remember, walking a golf course involves schlepping up and down five miles of hill and dale. If playing golf is the only exercise you get, you are likely to feel pretty wiped out by the back nine. This will likely detract from both your performance *and* your enjoyment of the game.

A while back, a patient came to me complaining that he felt listless and run down and that his love life was sub-par. I deftly told him that being out of shape may be his problem, and I recommended that he run five miles a day and see what happens. He called me a week later all excited.

"Doc, I took your advice. I've been running five miles a day and I feel like a million bucks!"

"Great!" I responded. "How's your love life?"

"Terrible, " he said. "I'm thirty-five miles from home!"

All kidding aside, it is imperative to keep in mind that aerobic training should be approached cautiously, and should be individualized for each golfer based on his or her age and the presence of underlying medical conditions such as high blood pressure and heart disease. *Golfers are advised to consult with their doctor before starting any vigorous exercise program.*

In summary, the ideal conditioning program for the recreational golfer should involve a progression of sport-specific activities designed to *develop muscular strength, endurance, flexibility of the muscles and joints used in golf, and overall aerobic fitness.* A successfully applied program can have many benefits for the golfer(65):

- No adverse effect on golfing performance (remember the first myth at the beginning of the chapter)
- Improved body composition (more lean body mass, reduced body fat)
- Improved control of blood pressure, glucose, and cholesterol
- Better joint and muscle flexibility
- Increased muscle strength—and increased club head speed!
- Lower risk of injury (not yet scientifically proven, but it makes sense to me)

Golf Exercises 101

When I decided to write this book, I knew I wanted to come up with something really unique. I hope that my experience as an orthopedic doctor and an average golfer has helped you, another average golfer, to come away with a real understanding of the hows and whys of musculoskeletal golf injury. The main focus of the book has been the injuries themselves. I think it's important for my readers, and for my patients, to have a solid understanding of *what's going wrong* before they can fix things.

You've heard me mention poor physical conditioning throughout the book as one of the major risk factors leading to injury among recreational golfers. There are dozens of golf fitness books already on the market—written by golf pros, athletic trainers, doctors, and other authorities (see Recommended Reading at the end of the book).

I hope you buy and read one of these books for two reasons. First, adhering to a basic golf conditioning program will likely decrease your risk for injury while increasing your performance and enjoyment of the game. Second, I don't have the space in this book to give the topic its proper coverage. This important subject is worthy of an entire book unto itself. In addition, there are numerous nationally franchised golf conditioning centers run by physical therapists or personal trainers who can perform a detailed analysis of your needs and tailor a program just for you (at a cost, of course). You can find such a facility near you by typing in "golf" and "fitness" on your Internet search engine.

Following are some basic strength, flexibility, and aerobic conditioning exercises that should help you get started on your way to better golf fitness. For these exercises, a "set" means the number of repetitions that can be performed without completely fatiguing the involved muscles (usually, eight to twelve repetitions a set is ideal). Use a weight that is challenging but not painful (a couple of pounds is usually sufficient). As strength increases, the number of repetitions per set as well as the number of sets performed per day can be gradually increased.

Keep in mind that strength training should not be done every day—not for the same muscles, anyway. The body needs at least one day between strengthening sessions for the muscles to recuperate. Flexibility and aerobic exercises can be done on the other days.

Strength Exercises
Shoulder and Chest

Modified Push-Up

This exercise is particularly helpful for developing strength in the pectoral muscles of the chest (the "pecs"), as well as the serratus anterior muscles of the shoulder blade.

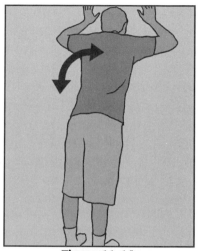

Figure 11-1A.
Modified push-up.

- Stand about two feet away from a wall, placing your arms straight ahead and palms flat against the wall. Standing on the balls of your feet, slowly lower your body forward to the wall until your upper arm is even with your shoulder joint. (Going any farther may overstretch the front part of the shoulder joint too much.) Now push yourself back as far as you can go. Hold, then repeat. Remember to keep your lower back straight during this exercise. (No sagging allowed!) For a more challenging exercise, a waist-high countertop or sturdy table can be used instead of a wall. Repeat to complete a full set.

Shoulder—Internal Rotation

Here's a good exercise for the important subscapularis muscle of the rotator cuff. Remember, research has shown that *both* shoulders contribute to the golf swing. Ignore the (incorrect) conventional wisdom that states that the left (lead) shoulder provides all the oomph to the golf swing.

• Lie on your right side in the fetal position with your hips and knees bent. With a dumbbell in your right hand, hold your right upper arm by your rib cage, and your forearm away from you against the floor.

Figure 11-1B. Shoulder internal rotation.

Now rotate the forearm so that the weight is brought up vertically to the chest. Slowly lower the weight to an inch or so from the floor and hold it there. Repeat to complete a full set. Switch to lying on your left side to exercise the left shoulder.

Shoulder—External Rotation

This exercise strengthens the supraspinatus and other external rotator muscles of the rotator cuff.

• Lie on your left side in the fetal position as above. This time, hold your right arm by your rib cage and bring your forearm across your belly.

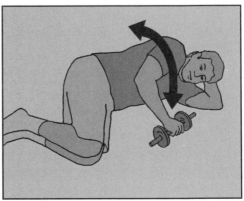

Figure 11-1C. Shoulder external rotation.

Hold the dumbbell in your right hand and rotate the weight off the ground, bringing your forearm as vertical as it will go. (Remember to keep your elbow against the rib cage.) Slowly bring the weight to the floor. Repeat to complete a full set. Switch sides to strengthen the left shoulder.

Shoulder—Extension

The latissimus dorsi muscles (the "lats") come into play during many sports activities, including throwing a ball and serving in tennis. In golf, the lats provide power during the downswing and accelerate the club head before impact.

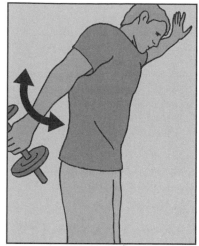

Figure 11-1D.
Shoulder extension.

- Stand about two feet or so away from a wall, feet flat on the ground. Lean forward, placing your left palm against the wall. Hold the dumbbell in your right hand and let your arm hang down. Now, slowly raise the dumbbell behind you while keeping your arm straight. When your arm is parallel to the ground, hold the weight there for a few seconds. Then slowly let the arm down. Repeat to complete a full set. Switch sides to strengthen the left lats.

Dumbbell Row

This is another good exercise for the important stabilizing muscles along the back of the shoulder blade. Weak scapular muscles rob the shoulder of a stable "platform" during the golf swing, making shoulder injury more likely.

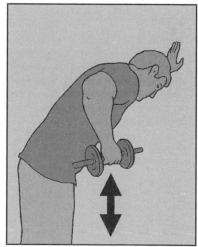

Figure 11-1E. Dumbbell row.

- Bend forward at the waist, and brace yourself against a table or bench with your left forearm. Hold the dumbbell in your right arm and let it hang down.

Now lift the weight up toward the ceiling, flexing the elbow as you go. Slowly let the weight back down. Repeat to complete a full set. Switch and do the left side.

Forearms and Hands

Wrist—Extension

Recall how common elbow injuries are among recreational golfers. Developing strong left wrist/forearm extensors will improve club stability at impact and should lessen the likelihood of developing common tendon injuries such as tennis elbow. The left elbow is particularly prone to extensor tendon injury at impact and at the top of the backswing.

- Sit in on a chair or bench with your left forearm on your thigh. Hold the dumbbell palm down just past your knee. Slowly extend your wrist while keeping your forearm on your thigh, and hold. Slowly let the

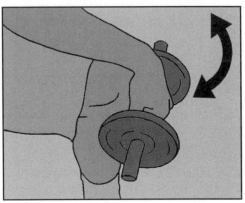

Figure 11-1F. Wrist extension.

weight down. Repeat to complete a full set. Don't forget to switch and strengthen the right side as well. (The right wrist/forearm extensors don't get stressed quite as much during the golf swing, but they do come in to play by helping to initiate the backswing.)

Wrist—Flexion

Golfer's elbow occurs as a result of injury to the common tendon of the wrist/forearm flexor muscles as it anchors into the inner portion of the elbow. The right elbow is usually at greatest risk for flexor tendon injury, especially at the impact phase and at the top of the backswing.

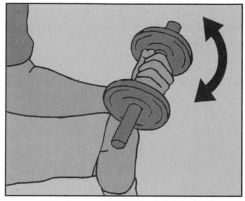

Figure 11-1G. Wrist flexion.

- Assume the same position as for the wrist extension exercise, but this time hold the dumbbell with the palm facing up. Flex (curl) the wrist as far as it will go, hold, and slowly let the weight back down. Repeat to complete a full set.

Grip Strengthening

Better grip strength will improve club control. There are lots of simple ways to strengthen the grip. One interesting fact is that the ring and pinky fingers are responsible for providing most of our grip strength.

- Squeezing a soft rubber ball is probably the simplest method of improving grip strength. Sports and health stores also sell latex bags filled with sand or squishy goo for the same purpose. The nice thing about this exercise is that you can do it just about any time. I keep one in the car. Even squeezing a sock will work, but make sure you remove your foot first! For this exercise, you can do a few dozen repetitions per set.

Trunk and Spine

Modified Sit-Up

A happy and healthy lower back depends on well-conditioned abdominal muscles. The abdominal muscles are a key secondary support to the lower back.

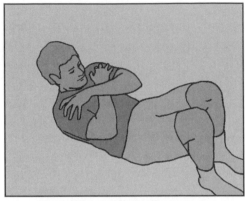

Figure 11-1H. Modified sit-up.

- Lie on your back with knees bent and feet flat on the floor. Hold your arms folded across your chest. Lift the head, neck, and shoulders so the upper back is off the floor while keeping the lower back in contact with the floor. Hold for a few seconds and slowly relax down. Repeat to complete a full set.

Modified Diagonal Sit-Up

This exercise helps strengthen the abdominal oblique muscles that help provide rotational control of the spine and help initiate the downswing.

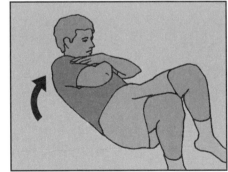

Figure 11-1I.
Modified diagonal sit-up.

- Lie on you back with your knees bent as in the Modified Sit-Up above, arms folded across the chest. Now lift your right shoulder off the floor and angle it diagonally toward your left hip. Hold the right shoulder blade off the floor for a few seconds, then relax. On the next repetition, raise the left shoulder and angle it to your right hip. Repeat to complete a full set.

Spine Extension

This routine helps strengthen the spinal extensor muscles of the lower back.

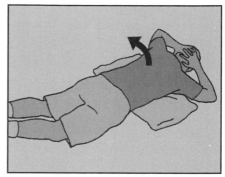

Figure 11-1J. Spine extension.

- Lie face down on the floor with a pillow under your pelvis and abdomen. Hold your hands behind your head and raise your chest a couple inches off the floor. Hold, and then slowly relax back down. Repeat to complete a full set.

Thighs and Legs

Modified Squat

Here's a simple exercise to strengthen the quadriceps muscles in the front of the thigh, and the gluteal muscles in the buttocks. The thigh and leg muscles are important for balance and power in the golf swing. Any successful baseball pitcher or hitter will attest to the importance of the legs for generating maximum power. The golf swing is no different.

Figure 11-1K.
Modified squat.

- Stand with your feet flat on the floor. Slowly assume a semi-squatting position and hold for five or ten seconds. Then slowly straighten up. Don't squat down too far—it's tough on the knees if your buttocks goes below your knees. Instead, pretend there's a chair behind you and keep your rear end about a foot off the imaginary chair at the lowest part of the squat.

Repeat to complete a full set. This exercise sounds silly, but I bet you'll be surprised how tough it is by the end of your first set.

Hip Extension

This exercise is good for the hamstring muscles in the back of the thigh.

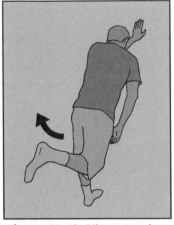

Figure 11-1L. Hip extension.

- You'll need something sturdy for support on this one. Brace yourself with your left hand. Place your weight on your left foot and lean forward though the hip. Steady yourself with your left hand as you extend your right leg behind you off the ground. Hold for ten seconds, then bring your leg back under you. Repeat to complete a full set. Do the same for the left leg.

Toe Raise

This exercise isolates the gastrocnemius muscles of the calves.

- Stand with your feet about 12 inches apart. Slowly rise up on the balls of your feet and hold for ten seconds or so, then slowly bring your heels back to the floor. You may want to stand near a wall to help you maintain your balance. Repeat to complete a full set. For a more challenging exercise, try rising up on one foot alone.

Flexibility Exercises

A basic golf stretching routine is outlined in the chapter on the golf warm-up. Going through the head-to-toe stretching sequence I describe there will make you a more flexible golfer. Unlike strengthening exercises, flexibility training can be performed daily. I recommend that you do some sort of flexibility training three to five times a week all year round.

In addition to the stretching exercises described in the warm-up routine, the following trunk rotation exercise is a great exercise for increasing flexibility in the back and trunk—probably the most critical body region for both golf performance and injury prevention. It also stretches the hips and chest. I did not include it in the regular warm-up routine because it's unlikely that many of you would actually lie down on the ground in front of your golfing buddies or business partners to do it. Instead, it's a great exercise to do in the privacy of your home or office:

Trunk Rotation

This exercise will help you increase the difference between the shoulder and hip turns on the backswing.

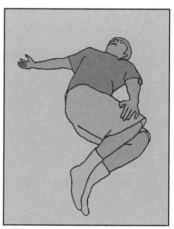

Figure 11-1M.
Trunk rotation.
(Illustrations 11-1 A-M
by Moki Kokoris)

- Lie on your left side in the fetal position. Hold your flexed knees to the floor with your left hand as you straighten your right arm and rotate your shoulders to the right. Try to rotate through your spine to bring your shoulders flat on the floor. (This is a tough exercise, so don't feel bad if you can't reach all the way back to the floor.) Hold this position for thirty seconds. Repeat while lying on the right side. Do this exercise five times for each side.

Aerobic Conditioning

To be considered an aerobic exercise, an activity must raise the heart rate to about 75 percent of a target "maximum heart rate" and keep it there for at least 20 minutes 3 times a week. A general formula for calculating the maximum heart rate (HR) is:

$$HR = 0.75 \times (220 - age)$$

For example, the target maximum heart rate for a forty- year-old would be 135 beats a minute. The 75 percent is a general rule of thumb. Golfers who are not in shape at all are better off aiming for a lower percentage of the target maximum heart rate (perhaps 60 percent for starters). Players who are in good shape already may aim for 80 percent of the target maximum heart rate. Under no circumstances should your heart rate ever exceed the "(220 – age)" part of the formula (66).

If you're anything like me, you probably approach the concept of aerobic fitness in a very unscientific manner. Every year or so, I decide that I am an overweight slob and get the urge to exercise. I'll get up early one day and jog a mile or two—which I *don't* do on a regular basis. After I finish throwing up my Wheaties I lie down until the fitness enthusiasm disappears. And it doesn't surface for another year.

I don't want to knock off my readers by getting you all gung-ho about exercise, only to have you harm yourselves. Previous fitness level—I'm sorry, but your being on the track team at Anytown High doesn't count for beans—your age, and your underlying medical conditions are all important factors to keep in mind when designing a sensible aerobic conditioning program. Achieving aerobic fitness will likely add to both your performance and your enjoyment of golf, but how you reach that goal is best planned by you and your doctor.

Parting Shots: Golf Conditioning

➤ Contrary to popular belief, strengthening and conditioning do not compromise flexibility and golf performance. In fact, research indicates that golf performance is *enhanced* by a basic flexibility and strengthening program.

➤ Another common misperception is that frequent playing can be a substitute for conditioning. You cannot play yourself into shape.

➤ A good golf fitness program addresses strength, flexibility, and basic aerobic conditioning.

➤ There are many "golf muscles" that contribute in a complicated and coordinated way to the golf swing. Each muscle group needs to be strengthened to have a safe, painless, and efficient swing.

➤ Because the golf swing stresses many joints, muscles, tendons, and ligaments to near all-out capacity, maintaining flexibility should be a main objective of the recreational golfer.

➤ Playing a round of golf on foot is equivalent to walking five miles and burns almost 1,000 calories. Basic aerobic conditioning can add increased endurance and enjoyment to the golfer's game.

➤ Because golfers come in all shapes, sizes, and levels of conditioning, they should consult their own physicians and tailor their conditioning routine to their own specific needs and capabilities.

➤ The numerous golf fitness books available provide detailed exercise programs that go beyond the basic information contained in this book. I encourage you to pick one up at your bookstore.

The Female Golfer

Females account for about one-quarter of the 25 million rec-reational golfers in the United States. Recently, I came across a thick medical book written exclusively about the female ath-lete. It was a very comprehensive book that covered every conceivable sport. I eagerly flipped to the chapter on golf, hop-ing to uncover some juicy new material. What I found, however, was the same material I was already familiar with.

The point here is that even though females are well repre-sented among the golfing population, there is surprisingly little research published in the medical literature that is dedicated specifically to the woman golfer.

Statistics about injuries among female golfers are available from some of the large surveys of professional and amateur golf-ers.

Golf Injuries in Professional Women

In one survey of members of the Ladies Professional Golf Association (LPGA), 99 members provided information about their golf-related injuries. The average age of these golfers was twenty-four years (range: twenty-two to forty-two years old), and there was an average of seventeen years golfing experience among them. During their careers, eighty-seven of the ninety-nine golfers (more than 80 percent) had been injured playing golf, and there were an average of two injuries per player.

The rate of injury among the women golfers was about the same as that of male professionals. The typical injury forced the female pro to miss almost three weeks from the Tour, compared with more than nine weeks for the men. However, some female players reported missing up to one year from competition due to their injuries (6).

The most frequently injured body areas among these female professionals were:

- Left wrist (31 percent of all injuries)
- Lower back (22 percent)
- Shoulder (8 percent)
- Left hand (8 percent)
- Left knee (6 percent)
- Left elbow (5 percent)
- Right wrist (5 percent)

The two most common *causes* for injury reported by this group of women professional golfers were:

- Overpractice / repetitive swings
- Contact with an object other than the ball during a swing (for example, the ground or a rock)

In summary, female professional golfers experience the same high injury rate that their male counterparts do. Overuse injuries, brought on by the relentless practice and play schedules these players maintain, predominate. These injuries can be nagging, resulting in weeks or months away from competition. Furthermore, more than half the women professionals reported that they are still bothered by their injuries (6).

GOLF INJURIES
Females

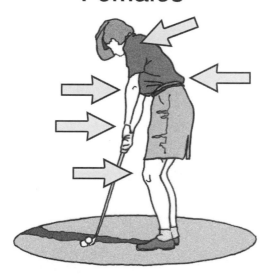

PROFESSIONAL	**AMATEUR**
WRIST / HAND (44%)	WRIST / HAND (15%)
LOW BACK (22%)	LOW BACK (27%)
SHOULDER (8%)	SHOULDER (16%)
ELBOW (7%)	ELBOW (36%)
KNEE (6%)	KNEE (11%)

Figure 12-1. Golf injures in females. This figure shows the most frequently reported sites of injury in a studies of professional and amateur female golfers who responded to two surveys (6)(4). (Illustration by Moki Kokoris)

Some important things to note:

- Injuries to the upper limb (shoulder, elbow, wrist, and hand) account for more than *half* of the total injuries, whether professional or amateur. The majority of these injuries occur to the left (lead) side.
- Injuries to the lower back are generally less frequent among females than males.
- The frequency of elbow injuries is much *higher* for the amateur player than it is for the professional. Professionals reported a much higher rate of wrist/hand injuries compared to amateurs
- Injuries to the lower limb (hip, knee, ankle and foot) are relatively uncommon for all female golfers.

Golf Injuries in Amateur Women

One published survey of amateur golfers included both men and women and provides some insight into the nature of golf injuries among females (4). The overall frequency of injuries was virtually the same for women and men—just over 60 percent for both sexes.

The most frequently injured body areas among these female amateurs were:

- Elbow (36 percent of all injuries)
- Lower back (27 percent)
- Shoulder (16 percent)
- Wrist/hand (15 percent)
- Knee (11 percent)

The three most common *causes* for injury reported by this group of women amateur golfers were:

- Excessive play/practice
- Poor swing mechanics
- Hitting the ground or an object during a swing

So, there are many similarities and a couple of differences in the injury patterns of male and female golfers. Women golfers, amateur and pro, run the same overall risk of injury as the men. The lead (left) side is most at risk for injury for all golfers, regardless of their skill level or gender. The overall pattern of distribution of injuries by body part is similar for females and males. One exception to this trend, however, is the disproportionately high rate of back injuries seen among men as compared with women. This is true for both professional and amateur golfers. Conversely, female golfers, amateur and pro, are more likely to sustain injuries to the upper limb (elbow, wrist, and hand) than male golfers (32).

There are couple of theories about why women hurt their backs less frequently than men:

- Male players, both amateur and pro, develop higher club velocity than the ladies and may rely more heavily on forceful trunk rotation during the downswing.

- Because by nature females possess greater trunk mobility than males, and therefore greater flexibility, females may be naturally protected against stressing their spines to their limits, resulting in fewer back injuries (32).

The few available studies that compare the muscle-firing patterns of females and males during the golf swing reveal a similar pattern for each gender. For example, Dr. Frank Jobe's research team has determined that female and male professional golfers exhibit essentially identical shoulder-muscle firing patterns during the golf swing (39). Admittedly, all the major muscle groups have yet to be compared between the sexes (the hips, for example, have not been fully studied).

If the biomechanics of the male and female golf swing are indeed similar, why, then, do men tend to hit the ball harder and farther than women? This is true both for the professional player (the average driving distance for the PGA Tour is about 250–300 yards, compared with 230–250 yards for the LPGA) and for the amateur golfer. There are a couple of reasons that this may be true:

- First and foremost, the average male is about 40 percent stronger than the average female (39). For example, the amateur world power-lifting record for thirty-year-old males is more than 450 kg, compared to about 275 kg for the females (63).
- Second, males tend to be taller, to have longer arms, and to use longer clubs than females—all of which contribute to a longer "lever arm" for the male golfer (39). I'll spare you the physics lesson, but suffice it to say that a longer lever arm results in greater club-head speed at impact, and hence greater distance.

I have my own theory why men hit the ball farther than women—because women are not burdened by the effects of that pesky male hormone testosterone. The women I've seen play are smart enough to know that hitting the ball *straight* is infinitely more important to achieving a respectable golf score than is hitting the ball *far*. I and millions of other male hackers often fall victim to the brief testosterone-fueled surge of euphoria that comes from crushing one. Our egos swell as our playing partners remark "Dang! You sure smacked the snot out of that one!" So what if it soars fifty yards past the green or into a lake, sand trap, or some guy's backyard—it sure looked good getting there.

The Older Female Golfer

Women are subject to the same age-related loss in muscle strength and performance as men. Studies of elite world-class athletes give us a better idea of how Father Time and Mother Nature conspire against the older female athlete (63):

- Muscle strength (the ability to perform short bursts of intense muscle activity, such as power-lifting) reaches a peak in females during their twenties. Muscle strength then declines rapidly (about 3.4 percent a year) through the mid-thirties. Beyond that, a slower but still steady decline in muscle strength (a decrease of 1.2 percent a year) continues for the next three decades.

- Muscle endurance (as measured by stationary rowing performance) reaches a peak during the thirties in females—compared with males, who peak in their twenties. From age thirty-five fifty-five, overall female muscle endurance declines slowly and gradually (about 5 percent over twenty years). Beyond age fifty-five, muscle endurance performance tails off more rapidly (nearly 1 percent a year).

In summary, when compared with their male counterparts, female elite athletes showed quite similar rates and patterns of decline in both muscle strength and endurance. Despite diligent training and conditioning through the years, these female athletes were still subject to a relentless decline in performance.

It is important to keep in mind that the average recreational golfer, female or male, is not a world-class athlete. Let's face it— as a group we're not in the best of shape. Therefore, with a *little* effort directed at proper conditioning, our performance could very well *improve* with time rather than decline. Two studies published in the medical literature showed that recreational golfers (female and male) who participated in a basic conditioning program for eight weeks achieved significant gains in muscle flexibility, strength, and club head speed (60)(65).

Osteoporosis

Osteoporosis is an important health issue facing all older females, including female golfers. As a bone doctor, I want you to be aware of this silent but potentially devastating disease. Osteoporosis occurs when the mineral (calcium) content of bone decreases over time, leading to weakened bones that are more susceptible to fracture. Females—especially women of Caucasian and Asian descent—are particularly prone to develop osteoporosis. Hip fractures are the most devastating consequence of osteoporosis. (There are more than 300,000 osteoporosis-related hip fractures in the United States each year, two-thirds of which occur in women.) Fractures of the spine, known as compression fractures, are also quite common, and there have been reports of women with osteoporosis who have suffered spinal fractures while playing golf (59).

I tell my patients to think of their bones as a calcium "bank account." We make "deposits" to the bank when we eat calcium-rich foods, and our bodies "withdraw" calcium from the bank to sustain important bodily functions. Up until age thirty-five or so, the amount of calcium in the bank account increases. It's as if we deposit ten dollars a day to our bank account while our body withdraws eight dollars. As women age, and particularly after menopause, the tide turns and the daily withdrawals from the calcium bank account slightly exceed the deposits. With time, the amount of calcium in the bone can fall to the point that the bones weaken and fracture from stresses, such as a golf swing, that would otherwise be tolerated by normal bone.

Unfortunately, there are no warning signs of osteoporosis. The disease is silent and painless until a fracture has occurred, and by then the proverbial horse is out of the barn.

As with most diseases, awareness and prevention of osteoporosis of is the smarter strategy. We get tested and treated for high blood pressure to ward off catastrophic heart attacks and strokes. Similarly, females at risk should be tested for osteoporosis to avoid painful and debilitating fractures later in life. —As an orthopedist I can promise you that a hip or spine fracture would keep the older female golfer from enjoying golf for a very long time—possibly forever.

Ask your family doctor, gynecologist, or orthopedist if you should be tested with a bone density scan. There are medications available to slow, and even reverse, the loss of bone calcium. Maintaining adequate dietary intake of calcium and vitamin D, performing regular weight-bearing exercise, such as golf, and avoiding smoking and excessive use of alcohol is a basic strategy that all women should adopt to ward off osteoporosis.

Parting Shots:
The Female Golfer

➤ Women make up about one-quarter of recreational golfers in the U.S.

➤ Injuries among professional female golfers are very common (greater than 80 percent). The rate of injuries among LPGA golfers is similar to that of PGA players, but women professional golfers suffer a higher frequency of injuries to the left wrist and hand, and fewer back injuries. Overpractice and mis-hits are the most common causes of injury among professional females

➤ Amateur female golfers get injured at about the same frequency as amateur men (about 60 percent). However, females tend to sustain fewer back injuries and more injuries to the left elbow, wrist, and hand.

➤ Excessive play and practice, poor swing mechanics, and mis-hits are the major causes of injury among amateur female golfers.

➤ The swing mechanics and muscle firing patterns seen in skilled female and male golfers are similar.

➤ Female athletes experience the same age-related decline in muscle performance—strength and endurance—as males. However, recreational female golfers have been shown to have significant increases in flexibility and strength by subscribing to a basic conditioning program. Golf performance, as measured by club head speed, also increased significantly as a result of a simple conditioning regimen.

➤ While there has not been much medical research dedicated specifically to the female golfer, the available information suggests that the sexes are quite similar when it comes to injuries in golf. Therefore, women golfers should adhere to the same basic guidelines as men:

—Keep in good physical condition.

—Avoid overuse from excessive play or practice.

—Warm up properly and adequately.

—Use good swing technique.

The Older Golfer

Golf is a unique sport in that it is actually *more* appealing to us as players as we get older. You don't see to many rugby leagues for folks in their Golden Years, but older golfers do represent some of the fastest growing segments of the golfing population (68). Studies show that there are about six million U.S. golfers over the age of fifty. Furthermore, while older golfers account for about one-quarter of all golfers, they play about *half* the total annual rounds in the United States (59).

For so many reasons, golf is quite popular among older players. The sport's unique handicap system allows for a "level" playing field, so that low and high handicap players, as well as younger and older players, can play together and still have fun "competing." Also, as we get older we tend to have more time. The kids no longer have Little League games on Saturday, and the workloads at our jobs tend to lighten up as the young bulls step in—all of which means more time for golf. Finally, we all know that playing golf isn't cheap, and older players may have the disposable income to make golf more affordable. Maybe life is fair after all.

All this sounds pretty rosy until you consider one fact: older golfers play golf with older bodies, and this can sometimes lead to problems. One survey of nearly 1,000 amateur golfers revealed that the injury rate was significantly higher for golfers over the age of fifty (65 percent injury rate) than it was for golfers younger than fifty (58 percent injury rate) (4).

Older golfers are not only more likely to be injured while playing golf, they are also more likely to have so-called incidental injuries—aches and pains from ailments that are not caused by golf but that nonetheless compromise golf performance, and enjoyment. For instance (5):

- Incidental back problems were reported by 52 percent of amateur golfers in one survey. The average age of these players with incidental back pain was fifty years.
- Twelve percent of the golfers had incidental knee ailments (average age, fifty-five).
- Nine percent reported hip problems (average age, sixty-two).
- Eight percent had incidental elbow pain (average age, forty-one).

None of this should come as a big surprise. We all carry with us the effects of years of wear and tear. Wouldn't it be nice if we could leave those ailments in the clubhouse locker along with our street shoes?

The Aging Process

Aging is a poorly understood phenomenon that affects all of the body's systems. The older golfer is not only more prone to injury but also tends to heal more slowly once injured.

Some of the changes we see in the aging individual are nervous system, cardiac system, and muscular system changes, and changes in the joints, the bones, and the spinal discs (70).

Nervous system changes. As we get older, the brain actually shrinks a bit (atrophy). The older brain gets less blood flow, and there is a decline in the available amount of chemical nerve transmitters. The speed with which our nerve impulses zip around our bodies decreases with time, resulting in reaction times that are about 20 percent slower in the older adult, compared with a younger adult. This probably explains why I recall driving with my grandfather to be such an adventure.

Cardiac system changes. Between ages thirty and seventy, cardiac output (the amount of blood the heart can pump per minute) declines by 30 percent. With age, the heart loses muscle mass, and the muscle fibers that remain do not contract as well (59).

Muscular system changes. A progressive decline in lean muscle mass and a replacement of muscle tissue with fat occurs throughout life. Both the number and size of our muscle fibers decrease with age. By age eighty, the body's muscle mass has shrunk by up to 30 percent, and muscle strength can drop by up to 50 percent between age thirty and eighty.

Joint changes. As we age, our joints literally wear out from a process known as *osteoarthritis.* The smooth (articular) cartilage that lines our joints changes in composition. Older cartilage loses its resiliency, making it less able to withstand stresses. The once smooth gliding surfaces of our joints become riddled with cracks and rough spots. In severe cases, the cartilage completely wears away, resulting in painful bone-on-bone contact. Joint flexibility can decline by up to 30 percent with age.

Bone changes. Men experience a 15 percent decline in bone mass by age seventy, whereas women lose twice that amount. Fractures become more commonplace, and in the older person fractured bones heal more slowly.

Spinal disc changes. The discs in our spines undergo perhaps the most dramatic age-related decline of any tissue in the body. As early as young adulthood, our discs begin to show tears and fissures. The water content of the spongy central core of the discs declines with age, and the discs lose their ability to absorb loads and stresses. The risk of disc herniation ("slipped" disc) increases with age.

Age-related degeneration also occurs in the muscles, ligaments, and joints that support the back, resulting in a spine that is less flexible and more susceptible to injury with age. In fact, older players exhibit about 50 percent less trunk rotational capacity than do younger or highly skilled players (32). This is one reason Richard, the patient whom I described in the chapter on back injuries, noticed he wasn't as flexible as he used to be. Trunk rotation, or lack thereof, is a major factor in determining club head speed. Too much twisting through a spine that has stiffened with age is also a good recipe for injury.

The Aging Elite Athlete

Even casual sports fans are aware that, for the most part, professional sports are for the young. The Sam Sneads and Nolan Ryans—athletes who effectively competed against players half their age—are few and far between.

One interesting study in the recent medical literature looked at the decline in peak performance in high-level athletes as they age (63). Specifically, two different types of athletic activity were analyzed. Muscle *endurance* was measured by stationary rowing capacity, and muscle *power* was measured by the weight that could be lifted in a single power lift. The amateur world records were then analyzed for various age-groups and for both sexes. The study revealed that:

- Muscle strength (power-lifting) performance peaks in an athlete's twenties, and rapidly declines during the thirties. A slower but steady decline in strength continues throughout the next five decades. The pattern of decline was similar for both males and females

- Muscle endurance (rowing) performance also peaked in the twenties, but it showed a more gradual decline from the twenties through the fifties. Endurance capacity declined most rapidly after age fifty-five. Women reached their peak endurance performance a little later in life (in their thirties) than the men, but showed a similar pattern of decline thereafter.

- Overall, aging seems to affect activities requiring short bursts of extreme muscle strength more than it affects endurance activities.
- Training alone is not enough to halt the inevitable negative effect that age has on this high level of athletic performance.

Professional golfers are not immune to the deterioration of their skills with time. A look back at the performances of nearly five hundred professionals competing from 1935 through 1997 revealed the following (75):

- Premier professional golfers reach their peak scoring ability at an average age of thirty-two, with a "peak range" between thirty and thirty-five.
- At age twenty, these golfers score about two and a half strokes higher per round than they do at their peak.
- By age fifty, their skills have declined such that they average almost three extra strokes per round.
- There were few elite professionals who managed to maintain their competitive edge into their fifties. Sam Snead and Don January were notable exceptions.

The Aging Amateur

If all these doom-and-gloom statistics about aging make you want to curl up on the couch and wait for the Grim Reaper, take heart. The fact is that a significant degree of age-related decline in body function can be slowed, and perhaps even prevented, by *regular exercise*. The fact that you're reading a golf book rather than one about the finer points of pinochle is a good start. It indicates that despite being older you are physically active and interested in staying that way. In fact, playing a round of golf on foot qualifies as a low-to-moderate aerobic exercise activity that may itself increase or maintain fitness and promote general health (72).

In some ways, we recreational golfers have it better than the pros when it comes to aging. For one thing, we don't have to rely on razor-sharp golf skills to put bread on the table, so the loss of a few shots here and there doesn't mean as much for us. Furthermore, few of us are in very good shape to begin with. With a little attention paid to conditioning and technique (lessons from a pro), most of us could probably make up for age-related losses of skill—and then some. Inactivity (disuse) is the main reason our muscle strength declines with age, and numerous studies have shown that regular exercise can result in dramatic improvement in strength in older adults (63).

The truth is that many golf medicine experts recommend strength training for golfers of all ages—especially the older golfer (59)(60)(65). The exercise regimens need not involve expensive gym equipment and personal trainers named Klaus. Home-based programs using light weights, rubber tubing, and so on, can work just fine.

To prove this point, seventeen recreational golfers with an average age of fifty-two were enrolled in a study to see if a modest exercise program would make a difference in golf performance (60). For eight weeks, the golfers attended twice-weekly conditioning classes for about an hour. The classes focused on light aerobics, stretching, and flexibility and strengthening exercises. All major body areas (legs, chest, trunk/abdomen, arms) received attention. When the golfers were retested at the end of the study, they all showed *significant* gains in muscle strength and flexibility. To make things even sweeter, their average club head speed increased by more than 6 percent!

A similar conditioning program with another group of senior golfers (average age, fifty-seven years) yielded equally encouraging benefits. The participants met three times a week for a basic strengthening and flexibility exercise program. After eight weeks, the golfers exhibited a decrease in body fat, a decrease in blood pressure, a greater than 50 percent increase in muscle strength, improved joint flexibility, and a five-mile-an-hour increase in club head speed—again, a 6 percent increase (65).

Is a decline in my golf game with age a foregone conclusion? And, if I play golf more and more as I get older, what can I do to prevent injury? These are among the big questions that are on the minds of older golfers.

On the first question, there is some good news. Golf skills for the amateur may not fall as dramatically with age as we fear. A survey of more than 1,300 golfers in England (74) revealed that handicaps improved by about one stroke a year up to age forty, and the rate of skill decline after age forty was surprisingly low: only 0.13 lost strokes a year. Beyond age seventy-five, the rate of decline in score was more rapid. (I know this must be a valid study because the English are much too honorable to fudge on their handicaps like we Yanks might be tempted to do.)

On the question of injury prevention, the recurrent theme in this chapter has been the importance of conditioning and regular exercise. While it is true that no scientific study to date has proven that regular conditioning prevents injury, or even improves scoring performance, it is the overwhelming consensus of all the experts that I've read that this is the case. Plus, it just makes good common sense.

One author put it best when he described the "foursome" of injury prevention strategies for the older golfer (59):

1. A stretching and strengthening exercise program, especially for the important rotational and stabilizing muscles of the spine and trunk
2. A conditioning program to build stamina and prevent fatigue
3. A full warm-up routine
4. Developing good swing habits with proper technique, tempo, and balance

A few years ago when my brother and I played a round of golf together while vacationing in Florida, we were paired up with a lovely older couple who must have been in their seventies. I remember thinking to myself, These folks are going to slow *us* down. I learned something about *age-ism* that day. Both those players not only beat us—they beat us *real badly.* Sure, I could hit the ball much farther than Mrs. Huffnagel could. But while I was trying to salvage my balls from among the prickly pears and alligator pits, she was quietly hitting the ball straight and true down the fairway. After that day, I never underestimated an older golfer.

Parting Shots:
The Older Golfer

➤ Golf is well suited for the older golfer for many reasons, but play should be approached with caution due to the higher injury rate and slower rate of healing seen in older players.

➤ Aging has a negative effect on almost all the body's major systems. Research has shown that the progression of age-related deterioration in the body can be slowed by regular exercise.

➤ High-level athletes face a distinct decline in muscle function, particularly peak muscle strength, by age thirty or so. Muscle endurance capacity also declines with age.

➤ Professional golfers typically experience a peak in performance during their thirties, followed by a gradual decline in skills.

➤ Older amateur golfers can significantly improve muscle strength, flexibility, and golf performance by adhering to a basic exercise program.

➤ Experts recommend that injury prevention in the older golfer include strategies to improve muscle strength, flexibility, and stamina, as well as adherence to a proper warm-up routine and good swing technique.

Joint Replacement and the Golfer

Golf appeals to me on many levels. One of the things I like most about the sport is being outdoors—away from phones and beepers. I also take comfort in knowing that, no matter how badly I fouled up on the previous hole, the next hole is started with a clean slate (Or, if you play with my brother, Gregg, and his fondness for Mulligans, then each hole is started with several clean slates).

To me, the main drawback of the game is the amount of time it takes (me) to play. I often feel guilty taking five or six hours on a weekend to play golf away from my wife and two small children—and then there's always the *back nine* to consider. I keep reminding myself that there will be plenty of time to play once the kids are grown and I retire.

Fortunately, the game of golf is ideally suited for the older player. I look forward to one day being one of those distinguished older gentlemen I see on the course—with their pants belted high above their bellybuttons—and their handicaps well below mine.

Unfortunately, older players can be afflicted with various medical conditions that might make playing painful or even dangerous. From an orthopedic point of view, arthritis of the hip, knee, and shoulder are common and painful problems that can ruin an otherwise good day of golf. Though not considered injuries in a technical sense, arthritis is common enough in the older golfer to warrant a general discussion here.

Arthritis affects millions of men and women each year. To keep things simple, we will limit our discussion to *osteoarthritis*—the age-related wear-and-tear degeneration of normal joint architecture.

Joints are beautifully designed devices in which silky smooth cartilage surfaces glide seamlessly over one another as we move our bodies. If we are fortunate enough to have both good luck and good genes, our joints can stay healthy and painless for life. More often, however, our joints begin to show signs of wear by the time we reach middle age. The normally frictionless cartilage layer lining the joint surface becomes damaged, leading to cracks, fissures, and flaking of the cartilage. Some joint surfaces can lose their cartilage cushion altogether, leading to painful bone-on-bone contact. Arthritic joints are typically painful, swollen, and stiff.

Osteoarthritis usually develops slowly, taking years to show symptoms and be visible on X-rays. Early complaints may include an ache or twinge of discomfort in the joint with activity or with weather changes. (No, your Aunt Sadie wasn't crazy when she used to announce at the dinner table that she could tell it was going to rain soon because her knees were acting up.) In its late stages, osteoarthritis of the hip, knee, or shoulder can render an otherwise healthy person unable to perform common daily activities such as walking, sleeping, or, heaven forbid, playing golf.

Evaluating a patient with osteoarthritis:

- Taking a thorough history helps rule out other common causes of arthritis. For example, a prior history of serious joint injury (post-traumatic arthritis) or previous joint infection (post-infectious arthritis) might be contributing to the problem. Inflammatory causes of arthritis, such as rheumatoid arthritis, should also be considered.
- Joints involved with osteoarthritis may be swollen, tender, and painful to move. With joint motion, there is often a clicking or grinding sensation.

- Depending on the severity of the arthritis, X-rays may appear normal, or they may reveal varying degrees of loss of the normal clear joint space occupied by cartilage in a healthy joint. In other words, even though cartilage is invisible on X-rays, the physician can make a diagnosis of arthritis if he or she sees on X-rays that the space where the cartilage lives is abnormally narrowed. So-called bone spurs are also frequently seen on X-rays of arthritic joints.

Nonsurgical, conservative treatment options for arthritic joints are numerous and are usually the first measures attempted:

- Rest or modification of activities (for example, taking up swimming to substitute for jogging on an arthritic knee)
- Weight loss, for hip and knee arthritis
- Anti-inflammatory medication (NSAIDs)
- Dietary supplements, such as glucosamine and chondroitin—nutrients purported to have cartilage-saving effects on arthritic joints
- Physical therapy to regain joint motion and strength
- Judicious use of cortisone injection into the affected joint(s)
- Injections of man-made lubricating fluid into the joint (particularly the knee)
- Bracing

For patients suffering from advanced arthritis that has not responded to nonsurgical measures, surgery may be the answer.

Arthroscopy, particularly of the knee or shoulder, can sometimes temporarily alleviate some of the pain by "cleaning out" the cartilage and bone debris in the joint. This is especially true in cases of mild arthritis. For severe arthritis, however, arthroscopy has not proven to be an effective long-term treatment.

Total joint replacement—prosthetic replacement of the arthritic hip, knee, or shoulder—is the ultimate surgical treatment for advanced arthritis. Simply put, a total joint prosthesis replaces the damaged joint surfaces (the knee hinge or the hip/

shoulder ball-and-socket) with a device made from various combinations of metal and polyethylene plastic.

The technology of joint prosthetics is rapidly evolving, with new and innovative designs being unveiled continuously. The particular prosthesis design chosen for a given patient depends on many factors, including the patient's age, weight, activity level, and the preferences of the surgeon. When successfully performed, a total joint replacement can have a wonderfully positive impact on a patient's quality of life.

While total joint replacement represents a great advance in medical science, it is important to remember that the replacement is not a *normal* joint, and that certain precautions need to be adhered to for life in order to minimize the risk of complications. Also, just like the brakes on your car, the materials in a joint prosthesis are subject to wear. The prosthesis can also loosen where it comes in contact with the bone. When a prosthesis loosens or wears out mechanically, it needs to be replaced ("revised"). Revision total joint surgery is technically demanding for the surgeon, and the outcome can be less rewarding for the patient than the initial joint replacement.

The goal, then, is to try to ensure that a patient's first prosthesis lasts for the rest of his or her life. Orthopedic surgeons and biomechanical researchers are continually trying to identify what factors hasten the loosening and/or mechanical failure of total joint prostheses.

Now we'll start talking golf again. Repetitive stress from heavy work or sports activities has been identified as contributing to premature failure of total joints (21). I'm sure I am not the only orthopedic surgeon who was concerned for the longevity of Bo Jackson's hip prosthesis when Bo announced he was returning to professional sports. The trick is to figure out which sports activities are "safe" for the long-term success of the joint replacement and which are threatening.

The key question for us golfers, then, is whether golf represents a "risky" behavior after a total hip, knee, or shoulder replacement. So far, the answer is encouraging.

Total Hip Replacement

Few if any, scientific studies have looked specifically at golf as it relates to early failure of a total hip prosthesis. Several studies have looked at the effects of various forms of recreational exercise after hip replacement, and golf has been included in some of these studies. When considered collectively, *moderate* forms of exercise, such as golf, swimming, biking, and walking, seem to have no ill consequences for the longevity of a hip prosthesis (17)(18)(21)(22).

What we do know about golf and total hip (and knee) replacements we owe largely to the work of Dr. William Mallon, a former golf pro and orthopedic surgeon who has written extensively in the medical literature about golf. Dr. Mallon conducted detailed surveys of experienced joint replacement surgeons, as well as of professional and amateur golfers who have undergone joint replacement surgery.

To get a surgeon's perspective, members of the Hip Society, which is a sort of orthopedic club made up of surgeons who are experts in hip replacement surgery, were asked their opinions regarding the role of golf and their hip replacement patients. The results of the survey should be a delight to sore-hipped golfers everywhere:

- None of these surgeons prohibited his patients from playing golf after hip replacement surgery.
- None of these surgeons reported that their golfing patients had higher complication rate than nongolfing patients.
- Many of these surgeons did recommend a three-to-four-month healing period after surgery before returning to play. Starting slowly with easy chipping and putting was recommended before returning to full swing play.
- About seven out of ten of these surgeons advised the use of a cart for their patients when they do resume play. (17)(18)(19)

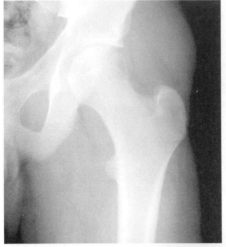

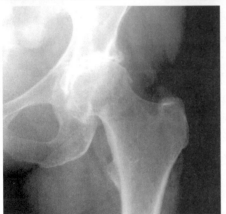

For the golfer's perspective, Dr. Mallon surveyed total hip recipients who were either golf pros or active amateurs who played at least three times a week. Fourteen pros and seventy-eight amateurs were included in the study (17)(18)(19).

- All the pros reported that they continued to play and teach after their surgery without problems.

- More than 90 percent of the amateurs responded that they had no hip pain when they played golf. All the remaining golfers who reported some degree of hip pain during golf noted that they still had less pain than they did before their hip replacement.

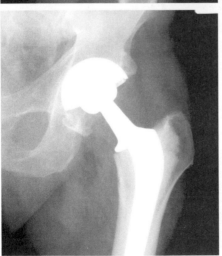

Figure 14-1. X-rays of a normal hip, an arthritic hip, and a total hip replacement. The first x-ray shows a normal hip joint with a clear space between the ball of the hip and the hip socket. This clear space is occupied by a layer of cushioning joint cartilage. In the arthritic hip (middle x-ray) the cartilage layer has worn away, resulting in painful bone-on-bone contact between the ball and socket. In the third x-ray, the arthritic bone and cartilage have been replaced with a metal and plastic prosthesis. (X-rays courtesy of Joel Buchalter MD)

- The players' handicaps were not changed significantly after total hip replacement surgery. So those of you out there who maintain that your bum hip is the only thing keeping you from being a walk-on invitee to the Senior Tour will have to come up with a new excuse—don't think that a shiny new hip joint will turn you into the Golden Bear.

Total Knee Replacement

An identical survey of the members of the Knee Society was conducted to evaluate how experienced knee replacement surgeons viewed our beloved sport. Again, the news was good:

- Some 93 percent of the surgeons responded that they did not object to their patients playing golf after knee replacement surgery. Seven percent suggested that their patients not return to golf.
- Each surgeon responded that every patient of theirs who expressed a desire to return to golf was able to do so after total knee replacement surgery.
- None of the surgeons reported a higher complication rate among patients who returned to golf after total knee replacement surgery.
- More than three-quarters of the surgeons recommended the use of golf carts after surgery.
- As with total hip replacement, at least three months of recovery time was advised postoperatively, before a gradual return to golf. A gradual and slow return to golf was recommended (17)(18)(20).

Total knee recipients, both professionals and serious amateurs, were also surveyed:

- The pros said they were able to play and teach golf unhindered by their total knee replacement.
- Some 90 percent of the amateurs were able to play golf without pain. The remaining players had some pain in their knee during golf, but less pain than they had before their surgery.

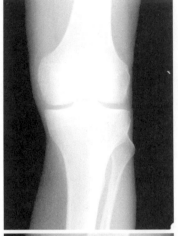

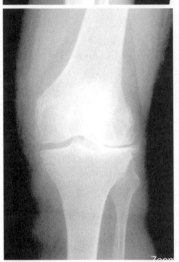

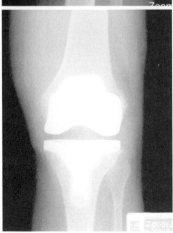

• The overall frequency of golf-related postoperative pain was higher in total knee replacement patients than it was for the hip replacement patients. Pain during golf was also noted to be more frequent in patients with a *left* knee replacement, which may be attributed to higher twisting stress on the left knee during the golf swing. (17)(18)(20)

The view is common among orthopedists that golf is an "accepted" sports activity after hip or knee replacement surgery. The Hip and Knee Society surveys, as well as a survey of doctors at the Mayo Clinic, each include golf on the recommended list of sports, along with such activities as cycling and swimming. Activities that were considered no-no's after hip or knee replacement included handball, racquetball, soccer, and basketball. (76).

Figure 14-2. X-rays of a normal knee, an arthritic knee, and a total knee replacement. The first x-ray shows a normal knee joint with a clear space between the thigh bone and the shin bone. This clear space is occupied by a layer of cushioning joint cartilage. In the arthritic knee (middle x-ray) the cartilage layer has worn away on the outer half of the joint, resulting in painful bone-on-bone contact. In the third x-ray, the arthritic bone and cartilage have been replaced with a metal and plastic prosthesis. (X-rays courtesy of Joel Buchalter MD)

Total Shoulder Replacement

Severe osteoarthritis of the shoulder occurs less frequently than that of the hip or knee, so consequently there are fewer golfers out there in need of total shoulder replacements. To date, there has been little research into the motion and stress demands that the golf swing places on the shoulder. Without supporting research data, it is difficult for surgeons to make informed recommendations to their patients about resuming golf after shoulder replacement surgery.

One recently published medical study did look closely at shoulder replacement surgery and the recreational golfer. Just as with hip and knee replacement, the relationship between golf and shoulder replacement seems to be a happy one. Members of the American Shoulder and Elbow Society were surveyed to learn what these experts feel about golf and shoulder replacement surgery (30).

- More than 90 percent of the surgeons encouraged their patients to return to golf.
- Some 60 percent of the surgeons placed no restrictions on how many rounds their patients could play each week.
- Some surgeons did express concern that golf may lead to premature wear and/or loosening of the components of the prosthesis.
- The average time recommended between surgery and a return to golf was four months.
- Half the doctors gave their golfing patients specific instructions about resuming play. They recommended that patients begin with putting and short shots before graduating to the longer irons. Furthermore, to avoid the stress that taking a divot might place on the shoulder, some doctors recommended teeing-up the ball, even on fairway shots.
- Some of the surgeons discouraged the use of a driver in order to reduce stress on the shoulder.
- About two-thirds of the experts felt it was all right for their patients to carry a golf bag while playing.

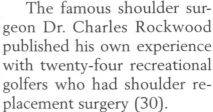

The famous shoulder surgeon Dr. Charles Rockwood published his own experience with twenty-four recreational golfers who had shoulder replacement surgery (30).

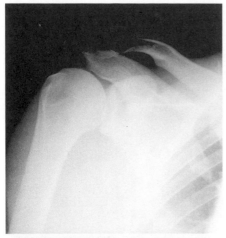

- Some 96 percent of these patients were able to return to recreational golf after shoulder replacement surgery. Patients who played golf after surgery experienced only an occasional mild shoulder ache after play.

- After surgery, patients were permitted to begin putting at two weeks, and chipping was allowed at four to six weeks. Medium-iron play resumed at six to eight weeks. The average time

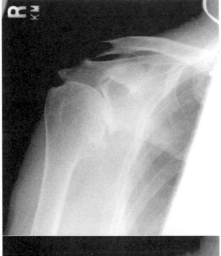

Figure 14-3. X-rays of a normal shoulder, an arthritic shoulder, and a total shoulder replacement. The first x-ray shows a normal shoulder joint with a clear space between the ball of the shoulder joint and the shoulder socket. This clear space is occupied by a layer of cushioning joint cartilage. In the arthritic shoulder (middle x-ray) the cartilage layer has worn away, resulting in painful bone-on-bone contact between the ball and socket. In the third X-ray, the arthritic bone and cartilage have been replaced with a metal and plastic prosthesis. (X-rays courtesy of Joel Buchalter MD)

between surgery and playing a full round of golf was four and a half months.

- Some patients reported improved scores after surgery— up to five strokes (Sign me up, Doc, I'd like to have *both* my shoulders replaced!)
- Dr. Rockwood recommended that his patients tee-up *all* shots for one year, to avoid the stress of taking a divot.
- After an average of four years follow-up, the postoperative complication rate, including prosthesis loosening, was the same when golfing patients were compared with a group of nongolfers who also had shoulder replacement.

Medical *theories* are transformed into medical *facts* when they pass the test of scientific scrutiny. For example, when a new drug is being examined for its safety and effectiveness, studies are proposed and planned, data are collected, and scientific analysis of the data is performed—before conclusions are drawn. The more participants that are involved in a study—for example, the patients taking an investigational medication—the more the conclusions drawn from the study are likely to be valid.

Similarly, conclusions drawn from scientific research are also more reliable if the studies are conducted over a long period of time. It may take years for an unexpected side-effect of a drug to become apparent.

Admittedly, the available surveys and studies linking golf and its effect on total joint replacement of the hip, knee, and shoulder are not supported by huge numbers of patients or decades of follow-up. Maybe some day we will have a Surgeon General who is both a golf nut and a total joint recipient. Then, perhaps a few zillion dollars can be allocated to do more in-depth research in golf medicine.

Until then, we can take comfort in the conclusions drawn from the studies that are now available: that golf seems to be a doctor-friendly, patient-friendly, and total-joint-friendly activity. I believe that golf hero Jack Nicklaus would be the first to proclaim the benefits of total joint surgery. Slowed by crippling arthritis of the left hip, the Golden Bear has again returned to the greens—with the help of a shiny new silver hip joint. Tom Nieporte, former Tour player and current head pro at Winged Foot Golf Club, also sings the praises of joint replacement surgery. Hampered by knee arthritis, Tom had both his knees replaced, and he returned to teaching and playing without missing a beat.

Total Joint Replacement and the Golf Swing

Okay, so we have surveys of world-famous orthopedic surgeons and their patients indicating that golf after total joint surgery does not appear to lead to increased complications or prosthesis failure. Still, total joint recipients should keep in mind that they need to take certain precautions for the rest of their lives in order to avoid unnecessary problems.

Advice from the Experts

As a result of his experience as both an expert golfer and an orthopedic surgeon, Dr. Mallon has published some general recommendations for patients who have undergone total joint replacement and who wish to continue to play golf (17). Recommendations from Dr. Rockwood, the shoulder expert, are also included (30). You, your physician, and your local golf pro should work as a *team* to tailor your game to meet your specific needs. Remember, too, that these guidelines are for *right-handed* golfers:

Pregame Preparation and Equipment Selection

- Avoid playing in wet weather or slippery conditions. A slip and fall could lead to a fracture around a joint prosthesis. That *would* be a *real* problem that you and your surgeon do *not* want to have.
- Playing without spikes may eliminate some of the stress on the hip or knee by allowing the feet to "slide" somewhat during the swing. Remember, though, to wear shoes that do provide adequate traction to reduce the chance of slipping and falling.

- Dr. Mallon points out that there is no scientific evidence to support the exclusive use of a golf cart after joint replacement. He has no objection to a player walking the course if it produces no pain. However, he cautions, *carrying a bag* may be too stressful for an artificial joint, and therefore he recommends the use of a pull-cart or a caddy.

The Address

- Adopting a more open stance, in which the golfer faces the target more, may benefit right-handed players who've had a left knee replacement. An open stance reduces the twisting stress on the left knee at impact and follow-through.

The Backswing

- Playing "on your toes" may be less stressful for a joint prosthesis than swinging flat-footed. On the backswing, the left heel rises off the turf. On the downswing, the right heel comes off the ground. The flat-footed swing advocated in golf magazine articles is really best suited only for younger players who are more flexible and have normal joints.

- Adopting a bigger hip turn may actually decrease the stress on a total hip prosthesis. Although this may not seem logical at first glance, Dr. Mallon points out that the hip turn is really performed by the lower back and trunk musculature. The more turning that occurs through the trunk, the less turning and stress is borne by the hip prosthesis. To make this concept work, however, the player must also adopt an "on your toes" swing technique.

- Making a bigger shoulder turn on the backswing may similarly decrease the stress on a shoulder replacement. This is true because the shoulder turn actually results from trunk rotation. Greater rotation through the trunk may translate to less stress on the shoulders and arms.

- Adopting a flatter swing plane, so that the ball is *swept* off the turf, may also decrease the stress on the shoulder.

The Impact

- Teeing-up the ball—even on fairway shots—can decrease the likelihood of taking a divot and will greatly decrease the force absorbed by the body at impact. This may be particularly useful for players who have had shoulder replacements. Recall Dr. Rockwood's recommendations that his total shoulder patients tee-up all shots for *one year* to avoid the stress of taking a divot. For those of you who don't like the idea of teeing-up every shot, playing "winter rules" may be a reasonable compromise. Under those rules, the lie of the ball can be improved without penalty.

The Follow-Through

- For the right-handed golfer with a right total knee replacement, *"stepping through" the golf shot* may be beneficial. Here, the right leg leaves the ground during the downswing and the follow-through, and the player steps toward the target. This shifts the weight, and stress, off the right knee. Note: Right-handed golfers with a left knee replacement should *not* adopt this technique.
- Kicking a golf cart or attempting to break a club shaft over one's knee places great stress on the hip and knee and should be avoided. (This one comes from me.)

Parting Shots:
Total Joint Replacement

➤ Total joint replacement of the hip, knee, or shoulder has become a safe and reliable option for the golfer afflicted with painful arthritis.

➤ Medical studies published to date indicate that golf may be a joint-friendly activity. Surveys of orthopedic surgeons reveal that the majority of doctors allow their total joint patients to return to golf after surgery, and that there does not appear to be a higher complication rate attributable to playing golf.

➤ All the experts surveyed recommended a gradual stepwise return to golf after surgery. Remember, golf is a demanding sport. Returning to full play too quickly will place undue stress on the player and on the prosthesis. Remember also that strength and flexibility in the rest of the body needs to be regained as well, before play can safely resume.

➤ If you are considering joint replacement surgery, let your surgeon know that you want to rcturn to playing golf after surgery. You could provide your doctor with copies of Dr. Mallon's and Rockwood's enlightening articles. Your surgeon may not be aware of these revealing studies. After reading them, your physician may feel much more comfortable giving you the green light to hit the greens again.

➤ Keep in mind that each patient is different and that a patient's postoperative activities must be addressed on a case-by-case basis. Together, I hope that you and your orthopedist can come up with a post-operative golf plan that you can *both* be happy with.

Golf Injury Roundup–
Putting It All Together

Pretend it's Sunday night. You've just spent the whole day watching one football game after another. For variety, you threw in some golf, tennis, and even a little hockey. Time for bed? Not a chance—there's still the sports highlight show.

This chapter is like that highlight show. I'm sure you already know this stuff for the most part, but hitting the high points one last time before I unleash you back on an unsuspecting public can't hurt. Remember, my primary goal is to keep you from getting injured.

General Comments About Golf Injuries

Golf injuries are extremely common to both amateur and professional players (about a sixty percent and eighty percent injury rate, respectively). Males and females have a similar risk of injury.

The main ingredients to the *amateur golfer's recipe for injury* are:

- Poor physical conditioning
- Overuse
- Inadequate or improper warm-up technique
- Poor swing technique

Professional golfers are at greatest risk for injury from overpractice and mis-hits. All golfers—pro or amateur, male or female—are at greater risk for injury with increasing age.

The majority of golf injuries occur over time due to overuse and poor swing technique. Each swing results in incremental trauma to the body. If the rate of this "microtrauma" exceeds the body's capacity for healing, a painful injury can result. Some injuries occur, however, as a result of trauma from a single bad shot (such as an ill-fated swipe at a ball sitting too close to a fixed object like a rock or tree root).

The main types of golf injuries are:
- Tendonitis (the most common injury type by far)
- Sprains (injury to ligaments)
- Strains (injury to muscle)
- Fractures (injury to bone)

Basic treatment guidelines for most tendonitis, sprain, and strain injuries include:
- Rest (eliminating—or at least minimizing—the activities that are causing the problem)
- Ice (to ease pain and calm down local inflammation)
- Anti-inflammatory medication
- Physical therapy (for chronic or nagging injuries)

Other treatments, including bracing, cortisone, and surgery,may be useful in selected cases.

The diagnosis and treatment of golf injuries is a team approach shared by doctors, physical therapists, and qualified teaching pros.
- Keep in mind that this book is not intended to replace your own doctor. Making the correct diagnosis requires good doctoring, and good doctoring requires someone who is skilled at taking a good history, performing a complete physical exam, and ordering appropriate diagnostic testing. ***Go see your doctor early, when the chance for getting simple and effective treatment is higher.***

- Physical therapy is a cornerstone of treatment for a myriad of golf related injuries, particularly tendonitis. Ask around for a therapy provider who has a special interest in golf rehabilitation (they are out there, I promise).

- The local golf pro actually wears two hats. (No, not one that says Top Flite and one that says Callaway, wise guy!) First, the golf pro can lend valuable advice to the golfer recovering from an injury by helping correct bad swing habits that may have contributed to the injury. Second— and more important—getting lessons from a pro before injury occurs may help *prevent* injury by correcting swing flaws before they can do damage. So, go get some golf lessons. You'll play better, and you'll be less likely to get hurt, to boot.

Basic conditioning and pre-play warm-up are two mainstays of golf injury prevention.

- Golf fitness entails a combination of exercises to improve strength, flexibility, and aerobic conditioning. Basic golf conditioning doesn't have to be elaborate, time consuming, or expensive. A modest investment of time and effort can pay handsome dividends—decreased risk of injury, increased enjoyment of the sport, and better golf performance. Remember those tenacious myths that say golfers lose flexibility when they perform strengthening (they don't) and that golfers can play themselves into shape (they can't). Finally, *remember to consult your own doctor before embarking on an exercise routine.*

- Few amateur golfers warm up properly, but all of us should. The warm-up is one area where the amateur athlete should aspire to be just like the professional. The key elements to a good golf warm-up include time, aerobic exercise, stretching, and progressive swinging. Decreased risk of injury and improved performance on the course are the rewards of a proper golf warm-up routine.

Common Golf Injuries—Symptoms, Treatments, and Golf Do's and Don'ts

Here's a recap of the most common injuries we learned about in the book, and some guidelines (do's and don'ts) to keep in mind when you are playing or taking your golf lesson (hint, hint). It goes without saying that a proper warm-up is a major "do" before every round or trip to the driving range.

Injury: Tennis elbow / golfer's elbow

Symptoms: Pain and tenderness on outer side of left elbow (tennis elbow) and inner side of right elbow (golfer's elbow). Pain may be greatest at the top of the backswing and at impact.

Treatment: Rest, medication, therapy, counterforce bracing, cortisone, surgery

Do:
- Consider switching to graphite shafts and low compression balls to decrease elbow strain at impact
- Practice on real turf instead of rubber mats when possible
- Ease up on grip pressure and loosen up on the elbows during the swing
- Bring the club back slowly during the backswing
- Maintain a smooth transition from the backswing to the downswing
- Move the ball to a safe spot to avoid contact with rocks, tree roots, sprinklers, etc
- Consider adopting a more elliptical swing to sweep the ball off the turf and minimize divot-taking
- Tee-up the ball on fairway shots, if necessary

Don't:
- Release the hands prematurely at the top of the backswing (casting maneuver)
- Decelerate the club *before* impact

Injury: DeQuervain's tendonitis

Symptoms: Pain, swelling,and tenderness at the wrist near the base of the thumb. Pain typically occurs at the left wrist at the top of the backswing

Treatment: Rest, medication, thumb spica splinting, therapy, cortisone, surgery

Do: Avoid excessive cocking of the left wrist at the top of the backswing

Don't: Release the hands prematurely at the top of the backswing (casting maneuver)

Note: Arthritis at the base of the thumb will produce symptoms very similar to those of DeQuervain's tendonitis. Your doctor can differentiate the two conditions by performing a careful physical exam and getting X-rays of the thumb.

Injury: ECU (extensor carpi ulnaris) tendonitis

Symptoms: Pain and tenderness over the inflamed tendon located near the knobby bump at the end of the ulna bone

Treatment: Rest, medication, splinting, cortisone, surgery (rarely)

Don't: Release the hands prematurely at the top of the backswing (casting maneuver)

Inury: ECU tendon subluxation

Symptoms: Painful clicking in the wrist near the knobby bump at the end of the ulna bone

Treatment: Casting, surgery to repair the torn tendon sheath

Do: Avoid taking fat shots and stay away from rocks, roots, etc.

Injury: Wrist impaction syndrome

Symptoms: Pain tenderness on the top of the wrist, usually on the right side at the top of the backswing

Treatment: Rest, splinting, cortisone, surgery (rarely)

Do: Slow down the backswing to minimize right wrist extension at the top of the backswing

---

Injury: Trigger finger

Symptoms: Painful locking and snapping of the finger

Treatment: Cortisone, surgery

Do:
- Use a glove to pad the more susceptible left hand
- Make sure that club handle grips are replaced as needed, or consider larger / softer grips
- Reduce grip pressure on the club handle
- Avoid the strong grip position by rotating the left hand counterclockwise

---

Injury: Fracture of hamate bone

Symptoms: Pain and tenderness in left palm, numbness in ring and pinky fingers

Treatment: Surgery, casting

Do: Make sure that your clubs are fitted properly so that the butt end of the club extends beyond the fleshy pad on the pinky-side of the left hand

Don't: Take fat shots or swing at balls near rocks, roots, or other obstructions

---

Injury: Carpal tunnel syndrome

Symptoms: Numbness and tingling of the fingers (particularly at night), hand weakness and clumsiness

Treatment: Rest, medication, splinting, surgery

Do:
- Make sure that club handle grips are replaced as needed, or consider larger / softer grips
- Reduce grip pressure on the club handle

Injury: Back pain
- Mechanical back pain
- Disc-related back pain
- Arthritis pain
- Stress fracture

Symptoms: Pain in back, stiffness, muscle spasm, leg symptoms if nerve irritation is present (numbness, pain, and / or weakness in the legs)

Treatment: Rest, medication, therapy, bracing, cortisone, surgery

Do:
- Use proper back mechanics when lifting your bag
- Bend through the knees (squat) when retrieving the ball
- Consider switching to a putter with a longer shaft
- Slow down the backswing to minimize rotational stress on the lower back at the top of the backswing
- Adopt a big shoulder and hip turn on the backswing (classic swing technique)
- Make sure body weight is properly shifted to the right foot during the backswing, and that the arms and shoulders are kept within the plane of the swing at the top of the backswing

Don't:
- Place the feet too far apart at the address phase (this limits the hip turn later in the swing and increases stress on the lower back)
- Hyperextend the spine on the follow-through, but rather utilize the relaxed upright "I" position (classic swing technique)

Injury: Shoulder pain
- Rotator cuff tendonitis, tear, impingement
- A-C joint arthritis
- Instability, scapular lag

Symptoms: Pain in the shoulder or upper arm at various phases of the golf swing, night pain, pain with overhead activities

Treatment: Rest, medication, therapy, cortisone, surgery

Do:
- Maintain proper strength and flexibility of the shoulder and scapular muscles (of *both* shoulders)
- Slow down the backswing to reduce stress on the shoulders
- Consider adopting a flatter swing plane to sweep the ball off the turf and reduce the change of shoulder-jolting divots

---

Injury: Knee pain
- Torn meniscus
- Knee arthritis (osteoarthritis)
- Kneecap pain (chondromalacia)

Symptoms: Pain, clicking, swelling of the knee aggravated by twisting, squatting, and walking

Treatment: Rest, medication, arthroscopic surgery (meniscus tear), total joint replacement surgery (severe arthritis), injection treatments, bracing, therapy

Do:
- Consider switching to spikeless shoes to reduce twisting stresses on the knees
- Focus on practice and play with short irons while recuperating from a knee injury (or surgery), to minimize stress on the knees

Don't:
- Return to full swinging prematurely after knee injury or surgery—the golf swing (especially when using a driver or long irons) places enough stress on the knee to risk re-injury

---

And there you have it. If you follow the guidelines in this book—get some lessons, start a basic conditioning program, and warm up thoroughly before you play—you are bound to play better, enjoy this great sport even more, and (with a little luck) avoid injury.

If you do get injured, you now have enough basic knowledge to work more closely with your doctor, therapist, and golf pro to solve the problem and get back out there.

Sometimes, despite all the preparation in the world, golf injuries can still occur.

"Doctor, I got stung by a bee while playing golf yesterday."

"Ouch," was the reply "Where did he sting you?"

"Between the first and second hole."

"Maybe you should keep your legs closer together when you swing!"

(Just another joke!)

You can help me and your fellow golfers out a lot by contacting me at my website:

www.doctordivotmd.com

There you will be able to tell me how to improve future editions of the book. (Sorry, the cornball humor is likely to stay!)My web site also has an interactive page where I answer queries from golfers like you. Perhaps you have a question about an injury not covered in the book. The site is also linked with suppliers of all sorts of golf-related goodies. If you own a golf-related business, you can order copies of this book at a discount to sell to your own customers. See you there!

Larry Foster, M.D.

RECOMMENDED READING

The publications listed below provide additional information that complements the contents of this book.

Exercise Guide to Better Golf by Frank W. Jobe, M.D. (published by Human Kinetics). This book is well illustrated, easy to read, and provides detailed flexibility and strengthening routines for the golfer. It even has tear-out reminder cards with the exercise routines on them to take with you to the golf course.

Golf Fit by Clay S. Harrow (published by Andrews & McMeel). This is another good fitness book that has many useful stretching and strengthening exercises for the golfer.

The Golf Doc by Ed Palank, M.D. (published by Jones & Bartlett Publishers). Dr. Palank, a cardiologist, has written a fun book that covers a wide range of golf-related health issues. There are chapters on cardiovascular fitness, nutrition, and even skin diseases common to the golfer, such as skin cancer and poison ivy.

Mind Over Golf: A Beginner's Guide to the Mental Game by Tom Nieporte and Don Sauers (published by e-reads). This book focuses on the psychology behind good golf. Surveys of top professional golfers give the reader an insight into what the pros do to gain the mental edge on the course.

Golf Injuries: Clinics in Sports Medicine, January 1996, edited by Gary N. Guten, M.D. (published by W. B. Saunders). Anyone with medical training (doctors, trainers, therapists) who wants to care for golfers should read this journal issue. It provided the scientific data behind much of the material discussed in my book, and more.

Feeling Up to Par: Medicine from Tee to Green, edited by Drs. Cornelius Stover, John McCarroll, and William Mallon (published by F. A. Davis). Another great book written for medical professionals. Besides discussing musculoskeletal injuries in detail, there are chapters on nutrition, cardiovascular health, vision, golf for the physically challenged, and much more. A must for any doctor who takes care of golfers.

Lowdown From the Lesson Tee, by David Glenz (published by Contemporary Books). A clearly-written and well-illustrated book about how to correct golf's most misunderstood teaching tips. From one of golf's most respected teachers.

REFERENCES

1. Hosea T, Gatt C: Back Pain in Golf. *Clinics in Sports Medicine* 15(1): 37–53, 1996.

2. Hosea T, Gatt C: Gertner E. Biomechanical Analysis of the Golfer's Back. In Stover CN, McCarroll JR, Mallon WL (eds.): *Feeling Up to Par: Medicine from Tee to Green.* Philadelphia: F. A. Davis, 1994.

3. Burdorf A, Van Der Steenhoven G, Tromp-Klaren E: A One-Year Prospective Study on Back Pain Among Novice Golfers. *American Journal of Sports Medicine* 24(5): 659–64, 1996.

4. McCarroll J, Rettig A, Shelbourne K: Injuries in the Amateur Golfer. *The Physician and Sports Medicine* 18(3): 122–26, 1990.

5. Batt M: A Survey of Golf Injuries in Amateur Golfers. *British Journal of Sports Medicine* 26(1): 63–65, 1992.

6. McCarroll J, Gioe T: Professional Golfers and the Price They Pay. *The Physician and Sports Medicine* 10(7): 64–70, 1982.

7. Stover C, Wiren G, Topaz S: The Modern Golf Swing and Stress Syndromes. *The Physician and Sports Medicine* 4(9): 42–47, 1976.

8. Plancher K, Halbrecht J, Lourie G: Medial and Lateral Epicondylitis in the Athlete. *Clinics in Sport Medicine* 15(2): 283–304, 1996.

9. Glazebrook M, Curwin S, Islam M, Kozey J, Stanish W: Medial Epicondylitis: An Electromyographic Analysis and an Investigation of Intervention Strategies. *American Journal of Sports Medicine* 22(5): 674–79, 1994.

10. Calahan T, Cooney W, Tamai K, Chao E: Biomechanics of the Golf Swing in Players with Pathologic Conditions of the Forearm, Wrist, and Hand. *American Journal of Sports Medicine* 19(3): 288–93, 1991.

11. Jobe F, Ciccotti M: Lateral and Medial Epicondylitis of the Elbow. *Journal of the American Academy of Orthopaedic Surgeons* 2(1): 1–8, 1994.

12. Armstrong N: Back Pain: Diagnosis and Treatment. In Stover CN, McCarroll JR, Mallon WJ (eds.): *Feeling Up to Par: Medicine from Tee to Green.* Philadelphia: F. A. Davis, 1994.

13. Stanish W, Loebenberg M, Kozey J: The Elbow. In Stover CN, McCarroll JR, Mallon WJ (eds.): *Feeling Up to Par: Medicine from Tee to Green.* Philadelphia: F. A. Davis, 1994.

14. Rettig A: The Wrist and Hand. In Stover CN, McCarroll JR, Mallon WJ (eds.): *Feeling Up to Par: Medicine from Tee to Green.* Philadelphia: F. A. Davis, 1994.

15. Torisu T: Fracture of the Hook of the Hamate by a Golfswing. *Clinical Orthopaedics and Related Research*, no. 83: 91–92, 1972.

16. Gupta A, Risitano G, Crawford R, Burke F: Fractures of the Hook of the Hamate. *Injury* 20:284–85, 1989.

17. Mallon W, The Golfer with a Total Joint Replacement. In Stover CN, McCarroll JR, Mallon WJ (eds.): *Feeling Up to Par: Medicine from Tee to Green.* Philadelphia: F. A. Davis, 1994.

18. Mallon W, Liebelt R, Mason J: Total Joint Replacement and Golf. *Clinics in Sports Medicine* 15(1): 179–90, 1996.

19. Mallon W, Callaghan J: Total Hip Arthroplasty in Active Golfers. *Journal of Arthroplasty* 7 supplement: 339–46, 1992.

20. Mallon W, Callaghan J: Total Knee Arthroplasty in Active Golfers. *Journal of Arthroplasty* 8(3), 1993.

21. Ritter M, Meding J: Total Hip Arthroplasty—Can the Patient Play Sports Again? *Orthopedics* 10 (10): 1447–52, 1987.

22. Dubs L, Gschwend N, Munzinger U: Sport After Total Hip Arthroplasty. *Archives of Orthopaedic and Traumatic Surgery* 101:161–69, 1983.

23. Carlstedt C, Nordin M: Biomechanics of Tendons and Ligaments. In Nordin M, Frankel V (eds.): *Basic Biomechanics of the Musculoskeletal System.* Philadelphia: Lea & Febiger, 1989.

24. Milford L: Carpal Tunnel and Ulnar Tunnel Syndromes and Stenosing Tenosynovitis. In Crenshaw A (ed.): *Campbell's Operative Orthopaedics* (7th ed.). St. Souis: C. V. Mosby Company, 1987.

25. Sauerland E: *Grant's Dissector* (7th ed.). Baltimore: Williams & Wilkins, 1984.

26. Murray P, Cooney W: Golf-Induced Injuries of the Wrist. *Clinics in Sports Medicine* 15(1): 85–109, 1996.

27. Posner M: Differential Diagnosis of Wrist Pain: Tendonitis, Ganglia, and Other Syndromes. In Peimer C (ed.): *Surgery of the Hand and Upper Extremity.* New York: McGraw-Hill, 1996.

28. Clancy W, Hagan S: Tendinitis in Golf. *Clinics in Sports Medicine* 15(1): 27–35, 1996.

29. Kohn H: Prevention and Treatment of Elbow Injuries in Golf. *Clinics in Sports Medicine* 15(1): 65–83, 1996.

30. Jensen K, Rockwood C: Shoulder Arthroplasty in Recreational Golfers. *Journal of Shoulder and Elbow Surgery* 7(4): 362–67, 1998.

31. Stover C, Mallon W: Golf Injuries: Treating the Play to Treat the Player. *Journal of Musculoskeletal Medicine,* 9(10): 55–72.

32. Theriault G, LaChance P: Golf Injuries—An Overview. *Sports Medicine* 26(1): 443–57, 1998.

33. Theriault G, Lacoste E, Gaboury M: Golf Injury Characteristics: A Survey from 528 Golfers. *Medicine and Science in Sports and Exercise* 28(5), 1996.

34. McCarroll J, Mallon W: Epidemiology of Golf Injuries. In Stover CN, McCarroll JR, Mallon WL (eds.): *Feeling Up to Par: Medicine from Tee to Green.* Philadelphia: F. A. Davis, 1994.

35. McCarroll J: The Frequency of Golf Injuries. *Clinics in Sports Medicine* 15(1): 1–7 , 1996.

36. Jobe F, Pink M: Shoulder Pain in Golf. *Clinics in Sports Medicine* 15(1): 55–63, 1996.

37. Andrews J, Whiteside J: The Shoulder. In Stover CN, McCarroll JR, Mallon WL (eds.): *Feeling Up to Par: Medicine from Tee to Green.* Philadelphia: F. A. Davis, 1994.

38. Jobe F, Moynes D, Antonelli D: Rotator Cuff Function During a Golf Swing. *American Journal of Sports Medicine* 14(5): 388–92, 1986.

39. Jobe F, Perry J, Pink M: Electromyographic Shoulder Activity in Men and Women Professional Golfers. *American Journal of Sports Medicine* 17(6): 782–87, 1989.

40. Zuckerman J, Matsen F: Biomechanics of the Shoulder. In Nordin M, Frankel V (eds.): *Basic Biomechanics of the Musculoskeletal System.* Philadelphia: Lea & Febiger, 1989.

41. Failla J: Differential Diagnosis of Hand Pain: Tendonitis, Ganglia, and Other Syndromes. In Peimer C (ed.): *Surgery of the Hand and Upper Extremity.* New York, McGraw-Hill, 1996.

42. North E, Kaul M: Compression Neuropathies: Median. In Peimer C (ed.): *Surgery of the Hand and Upper Extremity.* New York, McGraw-Hill, 1996.

43. Lindh M: Biomechanics of the Lumbar Spine. In Nordin M, Frankel V (eds.): *Basic Biomechanics of the Musculoskeletal System.* Philadelphia: Lea & Febiger, 1989.

44. Pitman M, Peterson L: Biomechanics of Skeletal Muscle. In Nordin M, Frankel V (eds.): *Basic Biomechanics of the Musculoskeletal System*. Philadelphia: Lea & Febiger, 1989.

45. Jenkins W, Callaway P, Malone T: Rehabilitation of the Injured Golfer. In Stover CN, McCarroll JR, Mallon WL (eds.): *Feeling Up to Par: Medicine from Tee to Green*. Philadelphia: F. A. Davis, 1994.

46. McCarroll J: The Lower Extremity. In Stover CN, McCarroll JR, Mallon WL (eds.): *Feeling Up to Par: Medicine from Tee to Green*. Philadelphia: F. A. Davis, 1994.

47. Guten G: Knee Injuries in Golf. *Clinics in Sports Medicine* 15(1): 111–28, 1996.

48. Vives M, Miller L, Rubenstein D, Taliwal R, Becker C: Repair of Rotator Cuff Tears in Golfers. *Arthroscopy: The Journal of Arthroscopic and Related Surgery* 17(2): 165–72, 2001.

49. Newcomer K, Laskowski E, Idank D, McLean T, Egan K: Corticosteroid Injection in Early Treatment of Lateral Epicondylitis. *Clinical Journal of Sports Medicine* 11(4): 214–22, 2001.

50. Noonan T, Garrett W: Muscle Strain Injury: Diagnosis and Treatment. *The Journal of the American Academy of Orthopaedic Surgeons* 7(4): 262–69, 1999.

51. Sinha A, Kaeding C, Wadley G: Upper Extremity Stress Fractures in Athletes: Clinical Features of 44 Cases. *Clinical Journal of Sports Medicine* 9(4): 199–202, 1999.

52. Haake M, Konig I, Decker T, Riedel C, Buch M, Muller H: Extracorporeal Shock Wave Therapy in the Treatment of Lateral Epicondylitis. *Journal of Bone and Joint Surgery* 84A(8), 2002 .

53. Adlington G: Proper Swing Technique and Biomechanics of Golf. *Clinics in Sports Medicine* 15(1): 9–26, 1996.

54. Gatt C, Pavol M, Parker R, Grabiner M: Three-Dimensional Knee Joint Kinetics During a Golf Swing. *American Journal of Sports Medicine* 26(2): 285–94, 1998.

55. Sugaya H, Tsuchiya A: Low Back Injury in Elite Professional Golfers: An Epidemiologic and Radiographic Study. In Farrally M, Cochran A (eds.): *Science and Golf III: Proceedings of the World Scientific Congress of Golf*. Champaign, Ill.: Human Kinetics, 1999.

56. Sanders S: Risk Factors in the Development and Management of Low Back Pain in Adults. In Rucker K, Cole A, Weinstein S (eds.): *Low Back Pain*. Oxford: Butterworth-Heineman, 2001.

57. Reinold M, Wilk K, Reed J, Crenshaw K, Andrews J: Interval Sports Programs: Guidelines for Baseball, Tennis, and Golf. *Journal of Orthopaedic and Sports Physical Therapy* 32(6): 293–98, 2002.

58. Deal D, Tipton J, Rosencrance E, Curl W, Smith T: Ice Reduces Edema. *Journal of Bone and Joint Surgery* 84A(9): 1573–78, , 2002 .

59. Lindsay D, Horton J, Vandervoort A: A Review of Injury Characteristics, Aging Factors and Prevention Programmes for the Older Golfer. *Sports Medicine*30(2): 89–103, 2000.

60. Hetu F, Christie C, Faigenbaum A: Effects of Conditioning on Physical Fitness and Club Head Speed in Mature Golfers. *Perceptual and Motor Skills* 86: 811–15, 1998.

61. Hetu F, Faigenbaum A: Conditioning for Golf: Guidelines for Safe and Effective Training. *Strength and Conditioning*, October 1996.

62. Fradkin A, Finch C, Sherman C: Warm-Up Practices of Golfers: Are They Adequate? *British Journal of Sports Medicine* 35:125–27, 2001.

63. Galloway M, Kadoko R, Jokl P: Effect of Aging on Male and Female Master Athletes' Performance in Strength Versus Endurance Activities. *American Journal of Orthopedics*, February 2000.

64. Jobe F, Schwab D: Golf for the Mature Athlete. *Clinics in Sports Medicine* 10(2): 269–82, 1991.

65. Westcott W, Dolan F, Cavicchi T: Golf and Strength Training are Compatible Activities. *Strength and Conditioning*, August 1996.

66. Pink M, Jobe F, Yocum L, Mottram R: Preventive Exercises in Golf: Arm, Leg, and Back. *Clinics in Sports Medicine* 15(1): 147–62, 1996.

67. Stover C, Stoltz J: Golf for the Senior Player. *Clinics in Sports Medicine* 15: 163, 1996.

68. Fleisig G: The Biomechanics of Golf. In Stover CN, McCarroll JR, Mallon WL (eds.): *Feeling Up to Par: Medicine from Tee to Green*. Philadelphia: F. A. Davis, 1994.

69. Mallon W: Training and Conditioning. In Stover CN, McCarroll JR, Mallon WL (eds.): *Feeling Up to Par: Medicine from Tee to Green*. Philadelphia: F. A. Davis, 1994.

70. Bostrum M, Buckwalter J: The Physiology of Aging. In Koval K (ed.): *Orthopaedic Knowledge Update 7: American Academy of Orthopaedic Surgeons*, Rosemont, Ill., 2002

71. Horton J, Lindsay D, Macintosh B: Abdominal Muscle Activation of Elite Male Golfers with Chronic Low Back Pain. *Medicine and Science in Sports and Exercise* 33(10): 1647–54, 2001.

72. Magnusson G: Golf—Exercise for Fitness and Health. In Farrally M, Cochran A (eds.): *Science and Golf III: Proceedings of the World Scientific Congress of Golf*. Champaign, Ill.: Human Kinetics, 1999.

73. Haller N, Haller D, Herbert D, Whalen T: A Multidisciplinary Approach to Performance Enhancement in the Aging Golfer: A Preliminary Study.

In Farrally M, Cochran A (eds.): *Science and Golf III: Proceedings of the World Scientific Congress of Golf.* Champaign, Ill.: Human Kinetics, 1999.

74. Lockwood J: A Small-Scale Local Survey of Age-Related Male Golfing Ability. In Farrally M, Cochran A (eds.): *Science and Golf III: Proceedings of the World Scientific Congress of Golf.* Champaign, Ill.: Human Kinetics, 1999.

75. Berry S, Larkey P: The Effects of Age on the Performance of Professional Golfers. In Farrally M, Cochran A (eds.): *Science and Golf III: Proceedings of the World Scientific Congress of Golf.* Champaign, Ill.: Human Kinetics, 1999.

76. Nicholls M, Selby J, Hartford J: Athletic Activity After Total Joint Replacement. *Orthopedics* 25(11): 1283–87, 2002.

77. Kibler W, McMullen J: Scapular Dyskinesis and Its Relation to Shoulder Pain. *Journal of the American Academy of Orthopaedic Surgeons* 11(2): 142–51, 2003.

INDEX

Page numbers in *italic* indicate information
contained in illustrations, figures, or captions.

A

abdominal oblique muscles, 151,160
acromio-clavicular joint (A-C joint),
    106, *107*, 112, 120, 208
address phase, 16, 50, 73, 101–102,
    135–136, 197
aerobic conditioning, 152–153, 163–
    164
age, and injuries
    aging process, 80, 178–180
    among amateur athletes, 181–184
    among women, 172–174
    elite athletes, 180–181
    frequency, 11
    shoulder problems, 112
amateur golfers
    aging and injuries, 181–184
    golf swing mechanics, and injuries,
        97–100
    injuries among women, 170–172
    injury frequency among, 11–13, *12*
    and warm-up, 139–140
Andrews, James, 116
anterior cruciate ligament (ACL), 124
anterior shoulder stretch, *145*
anti-inflammatory medications, 31–33
apprehension test, 115
Armstrong, Ned Brooks, 101
arthritis
    in A-C joint, 112, 120
    of lumbar spine, 90–91, 207
    osteoarthritis, 131–132, 186–188,
        208
    rheumatoid arthritis, 131
    and X-rays, 131
aspirin, 31–32

B

back injuries, 77–104
    and aging, 179–180
    among amateurs, 11
    among pros, 8–9, *10*, 78
    among women, *169*, 170
    arthritis of lumbar spine, 90–91,
        207
    disc-related back pain, *86–89*, 207
    mechanical back pain, 84–86, 207
    risk factors for, 82–84
    spine anatomy, 78–80, *79*
    stress fractures of lower back, 91–
        93, *92*, 207
    and swing mechanics, 80–82, *81*,
        97–100
    swing mechanics for avoiding,
        101–103
back strengthening exercises, *160–161*
back stretches, *145–146*
backswing phase, 17, 50–51, 73, 102,
    135–136, 197
basal joint, *56*
bending stress, *81*, 98–99, 101
bone fractures, *24–25*, 173–174
bone spurs, 112, *113*
bones, and aging, 173–174, 178–179

bracing/braces
    for elbow injuries, 43
    for knee osteoarthritis, 132
    for kneecap pain, 134
    for lumbar spine arthritis, 91, 92
bursitis, 112, *113*

C

calf strengthening exercise, 162
calf stretch, *147*
cardiac system, and aging, 178–179
carpal tunnel syndrome, 67–70, *69*, 206
casting maneuver, *51*, 73
casts, 66
chest strength exercises, *155–158*
chest stretch, *145*
chondromalacia (kneecap pain), 133–134, 208
clavicle, 106, *107*
club fitting, *72*, 75
club head speed, 4
cold therapy (cryotherapy), 28–29
collagen, 26
common extensor tendons, 39, *41*
common flexor tendons, 45, *47*
compression stress, *81*, 98, 126
computerized tomography (CT), 88
conditioning. *see* physical conditioning
cortisone
    about, 32–33
    for deQuervain's tendonitis, 59
    for disc herniation, 89
    for elbow tendonitis, 43–44, 48
    for osteoarthritis, 187
    for trigger finger, 65
cross-arm test, 115, 120

D

deltoid muscles, 107, 109, *110*
deQuervain's tendonitis, 57–60, 205
dietary supplements, 132, 187
discs, spinal
    and aging, 178–179
    herniation, *86*–89
Doctor Divot web site, 209
downswing phase, 17–18, *51*–52
dumbbell row, *157–158*

E

ECU tendon subluxation, 60–61, *62*
ECU tendonitis, 60, *62*, 205
elbow injuries, 35–54
    among amateurs, 11, *12*
    among women, *169*, 170
    elbow anatomy, *37*
    frequency of, 36, 45
    golfer's elbow, 45–49, *47*, 204
    risk factors for, 36
    swing mechanics for avoiding, 49–52, *51*
    tennis elbow, 39–45, *41*, 204
electrical stimulation, 29, 43
equipment selection
    club fitting, *72*, 75
    and joint replacement, 196–197
    and knee pain, 134–135
    putters, 101
erector spinae muscles, 151
Exercise Guide to Better Golf, 211
extensor muscles, 39–40
extracorporeal shock-wave treatment, 43

F

facet joints, 79, 90
Feeling up to Par—Medicine from Tee to Green, 50, 100–101, 116, 212
fingers. *see* trigger finger
Finkelstein test, *58*, 59
flexibility training, 151–152, 162–*163*. *see also* stretching
flexor muscles, 45–46
flexor tendonitis of the finger. *see* trigger finger
follow-through phase, 19, 74, 102–103, 198
forearm extensor muscles, 151
forearm flexor muscles, 151
forearm strengthening exercises, *158–159*
forearm stretch, *145*
fractures, bone, *24*–25
fractures, stress
    of lower back, 91–93, *92*, 207

G

Gatt, Charles, 97
gender, and injury rates, *10*, 11, 168, 170
Gertner, Eric, 97
Glenz, David, 212
gloves, 72
gluteal muscles, 151
The Golf Doc, 211
Golf Fit, 211
Golf Injuries: Clinics in Sports Medicine, 211
golfers. *see* amateur golfers; professional golfers; women golfers
golfer's elbow, 45–49, *47*, 204
graphite shafts, 50, 52
grip, golf, 63–*64*, *159*
grips, club, *72*
Guten, Gary, 134, 211

H

hamate bone, fracture of, *65*–67, 206
hamstring muscles, 151, 162
hamstring stretch, *146*
hand injuries. *see* wrist and hand injuries
hand therapy, 59
Harrow, Clay S., 211
heart rate, maximum, 163–164
hearts, and aging, 178–179
heat therapy, 29, 89
herniated discs, *86*–89
hip extension exercise, *162*
hip joint, 108
hip replacement, 189–191, *190*
Hosea, Timothy, 97
humerus, *37*, 106, *107*

I

ice treatment, 28–29
impact phase, 18–19, *49*, 52, 74, 198
impaction syndromes, 61, *62*, 206
impingement, shoulder, 112, *113*
impingement test, 115
injuries. *see also* specific injury types
and aging, 173–174, 177–178
causes of, 19–20

causes of, among amateurs, 13
causes of, among pros, 9, 168–*169*
causes of, among women, 168–*169*, 170–171
combination of factors for, 4–5
frequency of, among amateurs, 11–13, *12*
frequency of, among pros, 7–9, *10*, 167–*169*
frequency of, among women, 167–*169*, 170–171
and golf swing mechanics, 96
summary, 12–13, 201–202
Interval Sports Programs (ISP), 30–31
iontophoresis, 43

J

Jobe, Frank, 108, 171, 211
joints
and aging, 178–179
osteoarthritis, 186–188
swing mechanics and joint replacement, 196–198
total hip replacement, 189–191, *190*
total joint replacement, 187–188
total knee replacement, 191–*192*
total shoulder replacement, 193–195, *194*

K

knee injuries, 123–136
among women, *169*, 170
anatomy, 124–*125*
and equipment, 134–135
evaluation of, 127–128
knee mechanics during swing, 126
kneecap pain, 133–134, 208
meniscus tears, 128–*130*, 208
osteoarthritis, 131–132, 208
surgery, 132
treatments, 131–132
knee replacement, 191–*192*

L

lateral back stretch, *145*
lateral collateral ligament (LCL), 124

lateral epicondylitis. *see* tennis elbow
lateral meniscus, *125, 130*
lateral neck stretch, *144*
latissimus muscles, 107, 109, *110*, 151, 157
leg strengthening exercises, *161–162*
leg stretches, *146–147*
levator scapulae, 151
ligament sprains, *23–24*
Lowdown From the Lesson Tee, 212
lower back/trunk rotation stretch, *146*

M

magnetic resonance imaging (MRI), 88, 116, 129
Mallon, William, 189, 212
massage, 29
McCarroll, John, 212
medial collateral ligament (MCL), 124
medial epicondylitis. *see* golfer's elbow
medial meniscus tears, *125*, 128–*130*, 208
median nerve, *69*
medications, 31–33
meniscus, medial, tears, *125*, 128–*130*, 208
metacarpal bones, *56*
Mind Over Golf: A Beginner's Guide to the Mental Game, 141, 211
muscles/muscular system
    and aging, 178–179, 180
    key golf muscles, 151
    muscle soreness, delayed-onset, 21
    muscle strains, 21–23, *22*
    and warm-up, 20, 138
myelogram, 88

N

neck flexion stretch, *144*
neck rotation stretch, *144*
nervous system, and aging, 178–179
Nieporte, Tom, 140–142, 211
nonsteroidal anti-inflammatory drugs (NSAIDs)
    about, 31–32
    for carpal tunnel syndrome, 70
    for disc herniation, 89
    for elbow tendonitis, 42, 48
    for knee osteoarthritis, 132
    for kneecap pain, 134
    for mechanical back pain, 85

O

orthopedic surgical treatments. *see* surgical treatments
osteoarthritis, 131–132, 186–188, 208
osteoporosis, 173–174
overpractice, as cause of injury, 9
overuse, as contributing factor to injury, 20

P

Palank, Ed, 211
pars bone, 91, *92*
patella, 133–134
pectoral muscles, 107, 109, 151, 155
phalanges (finger bones), *56*
Phalen test, 69
phonophoresis, 29
physical conditioning, 149–164
    aerobic conditioning, 152–153, 163–164
    and aging, 181–184
    benefits of, 149–150
    components of, 19, 150
    flexibility, 151–152, 162–*163*
    strength, 150–151, *155–162*, 182
physical therapy
    about, 28–31
    for disc herniation, 89
    for elbow tendonitis, 42–43, 48
    for kneecap pain, 134
    for mechanical back pain, 85–86
    for osteoarthritis, 132, 187
    for shoulder injuries, 117
posterior cruciate ligament (PCL), 124
posterior shoulder stretch, *144*
practice schedules, 8
professional golfers
    aging, and injuries, 180–181
    golf swing mechanics, and injuries, 97–100
    injuries among women, 167–*169*
    injury frequency among, 7–9, *10*
    male and female injury differences, *10*

and warm-up, 140–142
push-up, modified, *155*

Q

quadriceps stretch, *147*
quadriceps tendon rupture, 124

R

radius, *37*, 55
range of motion (ROM) exercises, 29–30
referred pain, 87
rhomboid muscle, *110*, 151
rotation stress, *81*, 98, 126
rotator cuff injuries, 106–*107*, 109, 112–114, 118–120, 208. *see also* shoulder injuries
rotator cuff muscles, 151, 155, 156

S

Sauers, Don, 211
scapula, 106, *107*, *110*
scapular lag, *110*, 111, 120, 151, 208
scapular stabilizing muscles, 151, 157
serratus anterior muscles, 151
shear stress, *81*, 98, 126
shoes, spiked, 135
shoulder injuries, 105–122
    among amateurs, 11, 105–106
    among pros, 8–9, *10*, 105–106
    among women, *169*, 170
    anatomy, 106–108, *107*
    causes, 111–114, *113*
    diagnosing, 114–116
    muscle activity during swing, 108–111, *110*
    physical therapy, 117
    surgery, 118–120
    treatment, 116–117
    types, 112–114, 208
shoulder replacement, 193–195, *194*
shoulder strength exercises, *155–158*
shoulder stretches, *144–145*
sit-ups, modified, *160*
spinal nerves, 79, 80
spine extension exercise, *161*
spine injuries. *see* back injuries

splinting, 59, 66, 70
spondylolisthesis, *92*
sprains, ligament, 23–24
squat, modified, *161*
Stannish, William, 50
steroids, oral, 89
Stover, Cornelius, 212
strains, muscle, 21–23, *22*
strength training, 150–151, 182
strengthening exercises, 30, *155–162*
stress fracture, 25
stress fractures, of lower back, 91–93, *92*
stretching. *see also* flexibility training
    about, 138–139
    benefits, 151–152
    suggested stretches, 143–*147*, *144*, *145*, *146*
subscapularis muscle, 109
surgical treatments
    arthroscopy, 118, 187
    for carpal tunnel syndrome, 70
    for deQuervain's tendonitis, 59–60
    for disc herniation, 89
    for elbow tendonitis, 44–45, 48–49
    for hamate bone fracture, 66–67
    for meniscus tears, 130
    for osteoarthritis, 132, 187–188
    for shoulder injuries, 118–120
    for trigger finger, 65
swing mechanics
    avoiding back injuries, 101–103
    avoiding elbow tendonitis, 49–52, *51*
    avoiding wrist/hand injuries, 71–74, *72*
    and injury rates, 13, 20
    modern *vs.* classic techniques, 93–96, *94*, *95*, 102
    and total joint replacement, 196–198
swing phases, *15–19*

T

tendonitis
    about, 25–28, *26*
    cortisone for, 32–33, 43–44, 48

deQuervain's tendonitis, 57–60, 205

ECU tendonitis, 60, 62, 205

elbow tendonitis and swing mechanics, 49–52, 51

golfer's elbow, 45–49, 47, 204

rotator cuff, 113–114

tennis elbow, 39–45, 41, 204

trigger finger, 62–65, 63, 64

wrist flexor tendonitis, 61, 62

tennis elbow, 39–45, 41, 204

thigh strengthening exercises, 161–162

Tinel sign, 69

toe raise exercise, 162

toe touch stretch, 146

transcutaneous electrical nerve stimulation (TENS), 29

trapezius muscles, 110, 151

treatments
back pain, 85–86, 89
deQuervain's tendonitis, 59–60
golfer's elbow, 48
lumbar spine arthritis, 90–91
tennis elbow, 42–43

trigger finger, 62–65, 63, 64, 206

trunk flexibility exercise, 163

trunk strengthening exercises, 160–161

U

ulna, 37, 55

ulnar nerve, 47

ultrasound therapy, 29, 43, 89

V

vertebral bones, 78, 79

viscosupplementation, 132, 187

W

warm-up, 137–148
aerobic component, 143
and aging, 183
benefits, 137–139
frequency among amateurs, 139
and injury frequency, 20
and professional golfers, 140–142
progressive swinging, 147–148
stretching, 143–147, 144, 145, 146
time allotted, 143

women golfers, 167–174, 169

wrist and hand injuries, 55–75
among amateurs, 11, 12
among pros, 8–9, 10
among women, 169, 170
anatomy, 55–57, 56
carpal tunnel syndrome, 67–70, 69, 206
deQuervain's tendonitis, 57–60, 205
ECU tendon subluxation, 60–61, 62
ECU tendonitis, 60, 62, 205
hamate bone fracture, 65–67, 206
impaction syndromes, 61, 62, 206
swing mechanics for avoiding, 71–74, 72
trigger finger, 62–65, 63, 64, 206
wrist flexor tendonitis, 61

wrist flexor tendonitis, 61

wrist strengthening exercises, 158–159

wrist stretch, 145

X

x-rays, 59, 64, 66, 85, 88, 91, 116

Give the Gift of

Dr. Divot's Guide to Golf Injuries

to Your Friends and Colleagues

CHECK YOUR LEADING BOOKSTORE OR ORDER HERE

❑ **YES**, I want _____ copies of *Doctor Divot's Guide to Golf Injuries* at $19.95 each, plus $4.95 shipping per book (NY residents please add $1.40 sales tax per book). Canadian orders must be accompanied by a postal money order in U.S. funds. Allow 3-4 weeks for delivery.

❑ **YES**, I am interested in having Larry Foster, M.D., F.A.A.O.S. speak or give a seminar to my company, association, school, or organization. Please send information.

My check or money order for $_____ is enclosed.

Please charge my ❑ Visa ❑ MasterCard
❑ Discover ❑ American Express

Name _____

Organization _____

Address _____

City/State/Zip _____

Phone_____ E-mail _____

Card # _____

Exp. Date_____ Signature _____

Please make your check payable and return to:
Doctor Divot Publishing, Inc.
P.O. Box 436 • North Salem, NY 10560

Call your credit card order to: (800) 247-6553
Fax: (419) 281-6883